Kibblesworth

The Pearl on the Hillside

Dorothy A. Hall

JOHNSTON of KIBBLESWORTH

JOHNSTON OF KIBBLESWORTH.

William Johnston was living at Kibblesworth in 1666 when he was granted this Coat of Arms and Crest. The Head Teacher Bob Brown in 1993/4 based the Kibblesworth School badge on the Johnston Coat of Arms.

Previous page: These Deputies c1910 are standing in front of the screens at the Robert Pit, Kibblesworth.

The Robert Pit was the lifeblood of the village and in an age before the welfare state the livelihood of the villagers was reflected in the activity of the colliery. When the pit was idle or on short time life was hard in Kibblesworth.

Changing Kibblesworth,
Roy Dixon, Emmerson McMillan and Les Turnbull 1978 (1)

Copyright Dorothy A. Hall 2012

First published in 2012 by

Summerhill Books, Newcastle-upon-Tyne

www.summerhillbooks.co.uk   email: summerhillbooks@yahoo.co.uk

ISBN: 978-1-906721-57-2

CONTENTS

Internal photographs of miners' homes are rarely seen. This photograph shows George and Georgina Madden at their fireside, 34 Gardiner Square in the 1930s.

The huge blazing coal fire in the shining black and silver kitchen range, the big old busy kettle singing on the hob and the whispering gas lamps of a dark winter's evening provided memorable murmurings to set the scene for our family life during our early days in the mining village of Kibblesworth.   Doon the Waggon-Way, James W. Madden 1989

An aerial view of Kibblesworth Village in 1947.
(Photo Durham County Record Office CC/X 172/7)

Kibblesworth is a village whose type inspired the novels, poems and songs which have been written about the miner and his heritage. But unlike many of these villages Kibblesworth is still intact. The pit still wins coal, men step from the cage and while life races into the 1970s and pit shafts all over the country have ceased to work, "Kibb" remains a showcase on a mining community. The huge black pyramid of dirt which has been spewn out by the pit looms over the houses, chapel, club and street – a landmark for miles around. At the base of the pit heap a society with definite boundaries exists much in the same way as it did when coal was king.   Durham Chronicle, 8th October 1971 (3)

Introduction

In October 1986 I received a phone call which changed my life! The Head Teacher at Kibblesworth Primary School ('Where was Kibblesworth?') needed a supply teacher as soon as possible so getting instructions I drove to the village for the first time. Nineteen years later having driven that road twice every school day I retired from Kibblesworth – The Pearl on the Hillside. This title has been tucked away for over twenty five years. I met an old friend in Chester-le-Street and when I told her I was teaching at Kibblesworth, Mary Mossop said "Jack (her late husband born in the village) always called it "The Pearl on the Hillside". It stuck with me.

2012 is the fortieth anniversary of the opening of the "new school" and twenty years since the death of the man the School Staff called "Mac" and the village either Emmerson or Mr McMillan.

As always when you write books there are so many photographs and text you have to leave out. Much thought has gone into the choosing and there is usually a reason why each photograph is in the book.

Thank you all for your help and encouragement and big thank you to Alan, Claire, Gillian and Matthew who have had to put up with all the work that has gone into the actual writing of the book.

Dorothy A. Hall, October 2012

Mr Eddie Dewson and the pit pony (Kent) in front of the Robert Pit, Kibblesworth ready for the Centenary Blaydon Races Parade in 1962.

Chapter One
Ravensworth, Lamesley and Bewicke Main

John Nash (1752-1835) earned fame as an architect when he rebuilt Buckingham Palace, the great Pavilion at Brighton and for his reconstruction of Regent Street and Regent's Park in London. His services were obtained to rebuild

RAVENSWORTH CASTLE   GATESHEAD

Raveshelm Castle in 1807 and the noble edifice (seen here) came to grace our countryside.

Romantic Ravensworth, Clarence R. Walton 1950 (1)

The 1911 census was taken on the night of Sunday 2nd April. Each head of the household had to fill in the census form. Ravensworth Castle was no exception. Baron Ravensworth listed all his family and the servants resident at the Castle. There were six family members with two valets, four male servants, three sick nurses and eighteen female servants. There were sixty nine "rooms in the dwelling".

In the early days quite a number of collieries, and some private estates, paid for the personal use of a County policeman. The early Chief Constable Quarterly Reports usually list the appointments of such Constables as well as the regular recruits. The one on the photo appears to be such a constable who would be paid for by the Ravensworth Estate. That makes the photograph, to us, quite rare as we don't have many of 'additional policemen'. North East Police History Group

The 1911 census also records, living in the Castle grounds, the Head Gardener and his family and at "The Bothy" are six single gardeners living in four rooms. A large number of people worked on the Ravensworth Estate including Gamekeepers, Foresters, Joiners,  Masons, House Painters, an Estate Clerk of Works and a Land Agent.

Lady Park Lodge.

Ravensworth Castle has been leased by Miss Anderson of Gordon College Whitley Bay and will be opened in May as a residential school for girls. The castle affords accommodation for about 130 boarders. There is central heating, the drainage is thorough and modern and electric light is being installed throughout.
Newcastle Weekly Chronicle, 12th March 1921 (4)

Stately Ravensworth Castle may in the near future become a Poor Law Institution. A hundred inmates could be housed there without too much alteration.   Chester-le-Street Chronicle, 19th June 1931 (2)

(2) NORTHERN COMMAND TATTOO, RAVENSWORTH CASTLE, GATESHEAD.

Copyright
Andrew Reid & Co., Ltd.,
Newcastle upon Tyne.

The first Northern Command Tattoo took place at Ravensworth Castle in July 1934.

The attendance dropped from 87% to 47% this afternoon through so many parents taking their children to the rehearsal of the Military Tattoo at Ravensworth.

Kibblesworth School Log Book, 5th July 1934 (5)

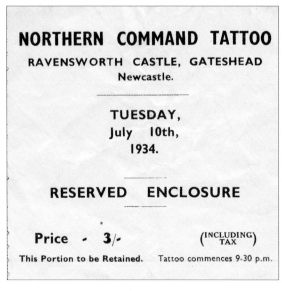

NORTHERN COMMAND TATTOO

RAVENSWORTH CASTLE, GATESHEAD
Newcastle.

TUESDAY,
July 10th,
1934.

RESERVED ENCLOSURE

Price - **3/-**   (INCLUDING TAX)

This Portion to be Retained.   Tattoo commences 9-30 p.m.

In the interval refreshments could be bought and there were a large number of tin baths containing lumps of ice in which bottles of Newcastle Brown nestled. On that warm summer evening at twilight the good old castle was floodlit. The buglers sounded lights out. As the searchlights ranged over the ground and the surrounding woodlands, we made our way home, happy in having had a beautiful day and an experience to be remembered.

Noel Miles of Springwell
writing to the Gateshead Post
1978 (3)

A second Tattoo was held in 1936 after which three thousand cushions went missing.

One letter received was from a man who returned eight cushions and stated that he did not discover them until he got home as they were accidently wrapped in a rug. As each cushion weighs two and a half pounds it shows that as a nation we are still powerful people.

Blaydon Courier,
8th August 1936 (3)

Mr Lewis Priestman of Shotley Bridge owned a coach and horses in the years before the Second World War. During the winter months the horses were stabled at Ravensworth Castle. Matt Elliott, seen here, was the postillion. The postillion rider normally rode the left horse of a pair (horses usually were trained only to be mounted from the left), to guide the horses pulling a carriage (especially a carriage without a coachman). Mr Priestman owned eighteen grey horses – all with names starting with the letter "V" – including: Valentine, Viking, Vandal, Veteran, Vivid, Viscount, Vandyke, Venture and Victor.

The seventh Lord Ravensworth decided in 1936 to pull the castle down as through the workings of a thirty acre coalfield beneath, the castle was beginning to sink and huge cracks were appearing in its walls. He intended to erect in its place a model village from the stone and valuable oak timbers. Today it is an empty shell and its hollow walls echo now only to the wind which rustles among its broken turrets or moans on wild nights through its empty windows.

Romantic Ravensworth, Clarence R. Walton 1950 (1)

Lamesley Church was rebuilt in 1759 and a plain square tower with an octagonal turret at the north east corner was added in 1821. The church consists of nave with narrow side aisles of equal height, each aisle formed by four obtusely pointed arches supported by lofty clustered pillars. The churchyard is spacious and adorned with trees.

History and Antiquities of the County Palatine of Durham,
W. Fordyce 1857 (1)

This country lane is now the busy road leading to the Team Valley Trading Estate.

North Eastern Trading Estates Ltd. was formed on May 18th 1936. Work was commenced on the site in September 1936. By May 1937, the month of the coronation of King George VI, the main road had reached this point and was named Kingsway. On July 29th 1937 this stone was laid by the Chairman of the Board of Directors Col. K.C. Appleyard O.B.E., J.P.
Stone at St George's House
Kingsway Team Valley

Rev. John and Mrs Emma Croft.

The Rev. John Croft was Vicar of Lamesley from 1898 until his death in 1951. In 1949 he fell from a ladder while pruning fruit trees and on his recovery began to read the New Testament through again in Greek. He was then ninety eight. In 1950 he and his wife celebrated their seventy fifth Wedding Anniversary. They are buried in Lamesley Churchyard.
The King's England Durham,
Arthur Mee 1953 (2)

11

George Symes when he was a choir boy at the Parish Church of St Andrew, Lamesley.

How easy it was to share in the cold Lenten services with the old Vicar and how impressive the Lessons were when read by Mr Corker. He also must have been a very old man in his eighties, but when he left his place in the choir stalls to stand at the gleaming golden eagle every eye was on him. He would return to his place wiping perspiration from his brow and we would stand to sing the canticles with all our might.
Doon the Waggon-Way,
James W. Madden 1989

Lamesley Church is appealing for more men and boys to join the church choir. Before the War says Mr H.F. Robson organist and choir master, the church had a strong and powerful choir of about twenty boys and a dozen men. Now the most that can be mustered are about a dozen altogether.
Gateshead Post, 3rd June 1949 (3)

On Friday last 200 children were allowed to spend the day in the grounds of Ravensworth Castle. The children left Lamesley at ten o'clock in the morning and after a most enjoyable walk along the private road through the park were shown over the extensive gardens. At three o'clock they had tea in the servants' hall and then returned to their sports. When it was almost dark they left the castle for their respective homes thoroughly well pleased with the day's entertainment.
Newcastle Courant, 19th September 1873 (4)

Lamesley School closed in 1943 and the building is now used as the Parish Hall for St Andrew's Church.

A view of
Lamesley from
The Willows.

*The area just
south of
Lamesley
Bridge is the
site of a
medieval
village.
A recent
archaeological
survey found
field patterns
of ridge and*

*furrow construction, field boundaries, flood defences and an ancient
track known as a hollow-way.*

Lamesley Pasture Information Board

The Alms houses were built in 1835 by Maria Susanna, Lady
Ravensworth in memory of her two children, for eight "poor and aged
females." The Alms houses were on the road to the Team Valley Trading
Estate near to the Roundabout on the A1 (M) and were demolished in
1967.

*The village of Lamesley is situated on a pleasant vale on the Team, to
the south west of Gateshead Fell and about four miles south of
Gateshead. It contains two public houses with a joiner's and
blacksmith's shop. The township abounds in excellent coal and the
various quarries yield a quantity of stone which is much used for
making grindstones.*   History and Antiquities of the County
Palatine of Durham, W. Fordyce 1857 (1)

Lamesley Station was opened in 1868 and was on the main railway line from Durham to Newcastle.

The Team valley branch of the North Eastern Railway passes through Lamesley and has a station about a quarter of a mile east of the village.
History, Topography and Directory of Durham, Whellan 1894 (1)

The station closed firstly to passengers on the 4th June 1945 and then closed entirely in 1959. The station buildings were demolished when the Tyne Marshalling Yard was built in the 1960s for the British Transport Commission.

Joseph Thompson and his wife Isabella with son William on her knee in about 1904.

There is seldom an English village without a blacksmith and Lamesley is no exception. William Thompson and his brother Cuthbert still ply their trade over the same anvil as their father and his father did in bygone days.
Romantic Ravensworth, Clarence R. Walton 1950
(1)

14

Cuthbert Thompson with his Shell petrol pumps. ICA stands for Ignition Control Additive which in a 1959 advertisement promised Shell users more miles to the gallon.

Chester-le-Street Rural District Council Meeting Report – Proposed Filling Station immediately North of Ravensworth Arms, Lamesley for Messrs Leech and Thompson – Approved subject to compliance with the requirements (if any) of the County Surveyor.
Chester-le-Street Chronicle,
23rd November 1938 (3)

The Ravensworth Arms, stands where once was Clubdon Hall, home of a branch of the Clavering family but only part of the original building now remains embodied in the present structure.
Romantic Ravensworth, Clarence R. Walton 1950 (1)

At the time my mother met my father she was working in an inn in Lamesley. She was working in the bar and had been for two or three years. My father, I understand, first set eyes on her when she served him in the saloon. Our Kate, Catherine Cookson 1969 (1)

Bewicke Main Colliery.

There was something special about Bewicke Main – something unplanned, unlikely and unpreserved made that ugly, dusty, doomed village into "a grand place". "It was hard but I'd go back tomorrow if it could be as it was before."
                    Bewicke Main 1862-1932, Unknown Author 1970s (3)

P.M. Church and Institute, Bewicke Main.   4055

This postcard shows Bewicke Main Institute on the left and the Primitive Methodist Church on the right. Until 1900 the Primitive Methodists used the School for their services.

The platform and harmonium have been removed and the Chapel folks have now ceased to use our premises. This is a great improvement to us and removing many inconveniences with which we have had to put up with for years. Bewicke Main School Log Book, 26th October 1900 (7)

The Bewicke Main School was built in 1873 by Birtley Iron Company.

School reopened this morning in the Primitive Chapel owing to the very bad and dangerous condition of the school due to pit workings.
Bewicke Main School Log Book 25th August 1931 (7)

The Schools, Bewicke Main. 4088

Mr Patterson the Head Teacher left at the end of September and on the 1st December 1931 the twenty nine children transferred to Kibblesworth School.

This is the view from High Row about 1912. The houses on the left are in The Square. A locomotive is marshalling wagons on the standard gauge railway line to Birtley while the narrow gauge wagonway from the Riding and the Mill Drifts on the right.

I have made a personal tour of Bewicke Main and have found conditions which are almost unbelievable. I was shown their dwellings many of which are propped up and after seeing the walls bulging ominously and showing large cracks I was glad to regain the open air. The windows are askew and the doors aslant to such an extent that considerable parts of them had to be cut away to make them open and shut.
Staff Reporter, Chester-le-Street Chronicle, 25th July 1930 (2)

An inquest was held at the Workingmen's Institute, Bewicke Main on Saturday concerning the death of David William Walker. A verdict of accidental death was recorded. The father of the deceased, Stephen Walker was also killed in this pit by a fall of stone. The

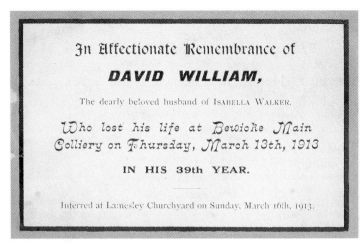

In Affectionate Remembrance of

DAVID WILLIAM,

The dearly beloved husband of ISABELLA WALKER,

Who lost his life at Bewicke Main Colliery on Thursday, March 13th, 1913

IN HIS 39th YEAR.

Interred at Lamesley Churchyard on Sunday, March 16th, 1913.

date of the accident was July 1st 1898 and his family was the first one in the County of Durham to obtain a grant under the Workmen's Compensation Act which came into operation that day.

Chester-le-Street Chronicle, 21st March 1913 (2)

The pit head with the Chapel on the left.

The whole of the remaining officials and workmen (numbering 128) of Bewicke Main Colliery will definitely cease work at the colliery on New Year's Eve. The majority of the workmen employed have spent the whole of their working life there.

Chester-le-Street Chronicle, 1st January 1932 (2)

Last weekend saw Bewicke Main completely derelict when the last of the residents moved out to new council houses at Kibblesworth. There is only one road in and that not much more than a bridle path.

Chester-le-Street Chronicle, 5th August 1939 (3)

Bewicke Main Lodge Banner, one of the three "Red" Banners in the North East, was purchased in 1924 at a cost of £60 from Tutill and Company. The portraits include Ramsay MacDonald, Keir Hardie M.P., Lenin, Mr Ben Oliver and Mr A.J. Cook. It had the radical motto "The Mines for the People" – an important political ambition of the Miners Federation of Great Britain. Before the banner was carried into the Durham Miners' Gala for the last time in 1929 the central picture of Ramsay MacDonald was painted over with white paint.

Banners in those days stood up to some hard times, many of them tattered and torn with broken poles, but stood repairing because £60 was regarded as a lot of money those days and to buy a new Banner meant a sixpence a fortnight levy to be collected from each mine worker at the time. Bewicke Main Banner Notes – Ned Cowen (1)

Mr Ben Oliver hopes to have a "miniature village" in operation at Bewicke Main at present just waste land. Mr Oliver has applied to the Rural District Council for permission to have a caravan site and light industry at Bewicke Main. The caravan village will have a Communal Hall and the present track road leading to the site will probably be converted into a concrete drive.

Durham Chronicle, 4th January 1957 (9)

Chapter Two
Kibblesworth

The first object that arrests the eye and attracts the footsteps of the wayfarer is an old fashioned public house (The Plough). Its tenant rejoices in the eminently Puritan name and Ultra Radical name of Ironsides – he is great in farming, butchering and an absolute monarch in the beer line.

Newcastle Weekly Chronicle, 18th April 1874 (4)

Before the mid 19th century Kibblesworth was a typical rural agricultural village. The nucleus of the village was The Hall, Plough Inn, village green and two farms at the eastern end of the present village. The settlement was mainly farm cottages and the residents were mainly farm labourers and village craftsmen.

Stephen Walker (6)

South Farm, on instructions from the Trustees of The Urpeth Estate, was sold in 1953 at the Lambton Arms Chester-le-Street. The Farmhouse (*below*) soundly constructed with slated roof, plus two recently modernised Farm cottages

(*above*), farm buildings with 147 acres were all offered for sale. East Farm was on the opposite side of the main road from Lamesley.

The Plough was moved to its present site in 1901. The Board is the name of the village's public house in 1856 but after that it is called The Plough. The Ravensworth estate originally owned both The Plough and The Ravensworth Arms. The latter was sold in 1921 and The Plough in 1933.

Provisional order granted for removal of licence to new premises about to be constructed on the south side of the main road. Confirmed by County Licensing Committee 17th October 1900. Final Order 14th August 1901.

Chester-le-Street Licences (8)

In 1180 Roger de Kibblesworth was the owner of the manor and vill of Kibblesworth which he held from the Bishop of Durham. In 1409 there is a record of a farmstead which is thought to be the present West Farm and Kibblesworth Hall is mentioned in the 1650s.

Stephen Walker (6)

Kibblesworth Hall a huge mass of brickwork is now known as The Barracks and is still a remarkable place. Today it gives very insufficient house room to twelve families of miners besides the village school and one of the two shops of which the community can boast.

Newcastle Weekly Chronicle, 18th April 1874 (4)

Hand franked postage stamp with Kibblesworth, Gateshead, 6th August 1917. The Post Office was on the ground floor of The Barracks from at least 1894. It was run for many years by members of the Forster family.

Kibblesworth Post Office removed from the Barracks to the The Square February 8th 1933.   Urwin Notebook (1)

The Barracks were demolished in 1934 and the very fine oak staircase, which at one time had been used by Oliver Cromwell, was removed by the architect E.M. Lawson to Kingston Gorse near Worthing, Sussex, to a house built for the London Palladium impresario George Black. It was afterwards the home of Billy Butlin.

Barrack Row before 1904.

A serious outbreak of fire occurred at Kibblesworth on Monday when four houses were completely gutted and a little child of seven burnt to death.   Durham Chronicle, 7th October 1904 (9)

Edward R. Middleton was burnt to death in his parents' house on Monday night – he was at school during the day.
                    Kibblesworth School Log Book, 7th October 1904 (5)

At a public meeting held in the Primitive Methodist Chapel Kibblesworth on the 6th the whole of the men offered to commence a subscription by paying 4 shillings a man and 2 shillings a boy to be kept off the pay at the colliery. The four families have been left quite destitute of home, food and clothing.   Durham Chronicle, 14th October 1904 (9)

A postcard view showing Coronation Terrace (built 1902) and part of The Square.

The colliery was located away from the village and the first colliery houses (Pit Row, Blue Row) were clustered round the pit. These houses were built of stone for the miners and their families. Barrack Terrace, Pond Row and the Pit Square were built later.

Stephen Walker (6)

In the winter, which appeared to be more severe in those days we had our favourite sledge runs across the fields, down the Pit Row or even down Kibblesworth Bank and through the village. Roads in those days were not salted so quickly and traffic not so frequent ... No married women worked and most single girls stayed at home to help their mothers. Some girls went into service. The officials at the colliery lived in The Crescent. They had servants – all girls from the village – who were paid two shilling (ten pence) a week. Yes they went every morning to do the washing and the cleaning and everything for two bob a week in the twenties and thirties.

Changing Kibblesworth,
Roy Dixon, Emmerson McMillan and Les Turnbull 1978 (1)

The Crescent was built in 1914. The Square at Spout Burn is on the right.

View from Kibblesworth Bank towards The Square.

The pit square was a feature common in mining settlements and its purpose was as a communal centre, the square was a centre of social activity and was a type of "industrial village green".

Stephen Walker (6)

West Farm is to the left of the photograph. In 1975 the farmland extended to 420 acres split between West Farm and Grange Farm to the south west of the village. The Rutherford family farmed here for many years. In 1934 David Askew became tenant and later in 1946 owner of the two farms. The Askew family still farm at Kibblesworth.

New branch premises of the Birtley Co-operative Society were opened on Saturday afternoon at Kibblesworth. The buildings costing £7000 are large and commodious for the sale of food stuff etc, drapery, wools, greengrocery and hardware, meat and boots all under one roof and on the market principle. Chester-le-Street Chronicle, 14th July 1922 (2)

Since the 1990s the Co-operative buildings have remained empty.

In the 1940s and 50s there was a Fish and Chip shop above the Co-op Stores. The newsagents was in a hut on the allotments behind Causey Row, later moving into Jack Woodhouse's "house shop" on the left. The Storey family afterwards took the

business over and modernised the shop. There was also a "house shop" in West View. The "Hadrian" shop was built on the site beside the Primitive Methodist Chapel.

When John Watson retires a nine decade link with the village post office will end. It started back in 1895 when Miss Annie Forster started the first village post office in The Barracks where Oliver Cromwell's troops lodged. Miss Foster handed over to her niece Miss Hunter in 1936 and she was postmistress until her niece took it over. That was Mr Watson's wife. Mr Watson has been sticking on the stamps and paying out the pensions for the last 27 years and he knows all the customers by name.
Evening Chronicle, 5th December 1979 (1)

In 2004 the Post Office, closed for over a year, opened in the general dealer store run by Paul Singh and his wife Balbier Kaur.

View from the colliery looking over the allotments to Laburnum Crescent with Gardiner Square on the left.

Our house was the third one from the top of the street. From the front door you could see the great big smoking pit chimney above the trees and the busy wheels of the pit head gear winding the heavy rope which lifted the cage and the miners out of the pit. On the other side of the house was the wagonway, the screens and all the pushing and shoving of the coal tubs and the cheerful joking of the miners going to work.
Doon the Waggon-Way, James W. Madden 1989

Ashvale Avenue and Laburnum Crescent were two streets of – sixty three Council Houses built in 1938 by the Chester-le-Street Rural District Council.

Chester-le-Street Rural District Council Meeting Report – A letter was read from Birtley District Co-operative Society Ltd. asking permission to hold a furniture exhibition in one of the houses at Kibblesworth for two weeks. Application was granted.

Chester-le-Street Chronicle, 28th January 1938 (3)

Chester-le-Street Rural District Council Meeting Report – Eighteen houses were now ready for occupation at Kibblesworth and the Lamesley Local Committee examined the list of probable tenants in accordance with the census taken at the time the slum clearance problem was dealt with.

Chester-le-Street Chronicle, 29th July 1938 (3)

Two of the three sides of Gardiner Square (built 1924) and the roofs of Grange Terrace (built 1915) can be seen here. The houses added on to the south side of Gardiner Square in 1963 can also be seen. In March 1996 a time capsule was buried in the Square.

The time capsule will remain underground for a period of thirty years. It is hoped (then) to examine its contents with a view to remembering and reminding the village of Kibblesworth of its past. In this case today will be the past. Time Capsule Flier 1996 (1)

The Square in the early years of the twentieth century had a communal bread oven and two open ash pits in the centre.

In 1939 out of the 1018 houses in Lamesley Parish 990 have a WC, 89 have ash closets and 33 have privies.
                    Rural District Council Medical Officer's Report 1939 (3)

In 1955 Causey Row and Pond Row were pulled down as was The Square in September 1967. About this time Low Row, High Row, Short Row and Pit Row were also demolished and the Grange Estate built in 1973 covered the area formerly occupied by Low and High Row.

The Square seen here with the bus stand and toilets to the front. In the 1960s the Northern number 79 bus travelled Chester-le-Street-Birtley-Lamesley-Kibblesworth hourly every day.

A village eyesore could soon be on the move if Gateshead councillors get their own way. Plans are now underway to demolish the bus shelter and public toilets at The Green Kibblesworth and build a new shelter. The toilets were bricked up in 1974 after repeated attacks by vandals.
                    Durham Chronicle, 11th December 1981 (3)

Rose Gardens – In the 1960s Chester-le-Street Rural District Council using Direct Labour, built a number of old people's bungalows on the site of Causey Row. Further bungalows were built after the demolition of The Square. In March 1971 Jack Craggs Chairman of the R.D.C. officially opened a block of twelve bungalows. Mr and Mrs W. Woodhouse were the first tenants.

Barrack Terrace was built on the site of Barrack Row after the fire in 1904.

During the Edwardian period (1900-1914) Durham prospered as a county and this was reflected in Kibblesworth. The newer colliery housing of this period differs from the older developments because builders began to use brick instead of stone.

Stephen Walker (6)

The great buff mansion is now dignified with the stolen title of Kibblesworth Hall. The original owner of this name – a name from which even the village old as it is was derived is now known as The Barracks.
Newcastle Weekly Chronicle, 18th April 1874. (4)

The twelfth century Kibblesworth Hall is being demolished to make way for a £100,000 housing scheme. The Hall, home of Sir Roger de Kibble and the famous County Durham family of Greenwell has remained the biggest and most imposing house in the village of Kibblesworth to which it gave its name. Northern Echo, 30th April 1973 (1)

The Hall stood away from the main road, commanded an extensive view and was surrounded by four acres of gardens. Many of the Colliery Managers lived here as it was owned by John Bowes and Partners. From the late 1930s it was the home of Robert and Blanche Thompson. After their deaths the Hall was sold and demolished in May 1973. The Woodlands housing estate was built on the land.

Kibblesworth will be a forgotten village when its last claim to history is pulled down. The Civic Trust for the North-East said yesterday the village could be written off as far as history was concerned now that the Hall was doomed. The roof has been pulled off and the old fireplaces taken out. Only the bare walls are left.
Northern Echo, 1st May 1973 (1)

Schoolgirl Andrea Morgan is helping build a little bit of history in Kibblesworth. She persuaded her uncle (Stewart Clarke of No Place) to lend a hand making a unique memorial with some bricks salvaged from the demolished Kibblesworth Hall.

Evening Chronicle,
5th December 1979
(1)

The Brass plaque read:

These handmade bricks came from Kibblesworth Old Hall c1180. Oliver

Cromwell reputedly stayed here in 1647.

The school bought a Pit Tub £1 and a stanchion from the colliery which recently closed down.

Kibblesworth School Log Book, 11th July 1975 (5)

The Plaque read: Kibblesworth Colliery 1842-1974.

Liddell Terrace – a reminder of the Ravensworths whose family name was Liddell.

During the early years of the twentieth century Kibblesworth Colliery continued to prosper and this is reflected in further housing development – Coronation Terrace (1902), Prospect Terrace (1908), The Crescent (1914). During this period private housing was developed and these included West View, Liddell Terrace and the development of villas at the east end of the village.   Stephen Walker (6)

Everything which epitomises the Geordie miner can be found in Kibblesworth – the club, surely one of the biggest in the area, the dogs, the allotments, the gardens and the pigeons.

Durham Chronicle, 8th October 1971 (3)

The flats on Greenford.

The Durham County development plan in 1951 placed Kibblesworth in category "B" because it expected local employment for men living in these communities would continue into the future. This plan allowed development at Kibblesworth and in 1954-5 over two hundred houses were built at Moormill, Greenford, Ouselaw and Coltspool.   Stephen Walker (6)

Picture hanging – Nails must not be driven into walls. Special hangers are readily available for the hanging of pictures, mirrors etc

Chester-le-Street R.D.C. Tenants Handbook 1959 (2)

Moormill.

The Airey house is in every way as strong as a brick building. The shell is of concrete and the inside of breeze or hollow blocks. The cost is from £290 to £300 more than the traditional brick house. The Airey houses are extremely pleasant in appearance and very substantial.

Durham Rural District Council Meeting
Durham Chronicle, 23rd August 1946 (9)

Tenants are reminded that as ratepayers they are part owners of the housing estates and it is in their own interests to maintain and preserve the property.

Chester-le-Street R.D.C. Tenants Handbook 1959 (2)

In March 2010 Gateshead Council granted permission for nearly 150 new houses to be built at Kibblesworth on the Moormill, Coltspool Greenford and Ouselaw estate.

A block of four Airey houses from Kibblesworth is being painstakingly deconstructed, loaded onto pallets and transported to Beamish Museum. Prefabs were a quick solution to the housing crisis in the aftermath of

the Second World War. The houses a type of prefabricated dwelling were designed by Sir Edwin Airey and featured a frame of prefabricated concrete columns clad with a series of ship lap style concrete panels. The terrace of four houses appears to be peculiar to the North East.

Evening Chronicle,
4th May 2012 (1)

Chapter Three
The Colliery

The Robert Pit is carried on by Messrs John Bowes and Partners Limited, working the Low Main fifty five fathoms deep and the Hutton sixty fathoms. The former varies from three to six feet the  *Hutton seam is about four foot two inches.*

History, Topography and Directory of Durham, Whellan 1894 (1)

The pit head, the engine house is on the left, the head gear in the centre is above the shaft behind which are the screens for sorting the coal; the other buildings are workshops.

The shaft is ten foot six inches diameter lined with brick and stone. The shaft is fitted with wood guides and the double deck cages carry two wood tubs one in each deck each tub carrying eight and a quarter hundred weights of coal. The shaft headgear is of steel girders with winding pulleys ten feet in diameter.

National Coal Board Report on Kibblesworth Colliery, No Date (1)

The Robert Pit used candles not pit lamps as unlike the Glamis it had no problems with gas.

Kibblesworth Colliery.

An essential article for the miner was candles. He had to supply his own for use down the pit. Broughs sold a lot of wax candles in various sizes, 12's and 18's were always on order sold in 3lb packets and of course there would be three dozen boxes of matches for 4d.

Broughs Limited, H.G. Ellis c1948 (2)

Hewers. The fore shift hewers shall descend at 4am and be loosed by their marrows in the face to ride at 11am. The back shift shall descend at 9.30am and commence to ride at 4.30pm.

Kibblesworth Lodge Agreement, 12th August 1915 (10)

On Wednesday morning about 8 o'clock the village of Kibblesworth was suddenly alarmed by a terrific noise proceeding from the colliery a few yards distant. At first it was thought the pit head had fired but on the smoke and steam clearing away it was ascertained that one of the boilers had exploded destroying one man and seriously scalding and injuring several others. Newcastle Courant, 21st September 1855 (4)

In 1844 34,000 miners were employed in the Northumberland and Durham Coalfield. In 1873 the figures had risen to about 77,000. In 1913 there were 227.000 miners employed producing 56.4 million tons of coal. After this high point the numbers drop to 160,000 in 1938, 149,000 in 1948 and in 1980 36,000. Today (2012) there are no deep coal miners employed in Northumberland and Durham.

High Speed Mining Pump number 474 made by Andrew Barclay, Sons and Co Ltd of Caledonia Works Kilmarnock.

Recently at Kibblesworth colliery great developments have taken place – the erection of a fan on the most approved principle for the purpose of extracting the foul air from the pit. This takes the place of the old fashioned furnace which has done duty ever since the colliery began. Durham Chronicle, 15th June 1906 (9)

In 1914 the Kibblesworth Grange Drift mine was opened to work the Five Quarter seam. In 1929 the Robert Pit employed 519 men with the Grange Drift employing another 274 men. In 1932 the Grange Drift was closed but this was largely offset by the opening in 1934 of the Dorothy Drift to mine the High Main seam. Stephen Walker (6)

The Colliery Offices, Grange Terrace were built in 1921 before this miners' pay was collected from The Cottage opposite the Wesleyan Chapel.

Up to the time of the Great War the wages of the miners had been paid fortnightly but the men had for long been agitating for a weekly pay packet and at last change began to take place. It was no use sending goods on a Friday to places where the wages were not paid until Saturday noon. Generally speaking there was no money in the houses a day or two prior to pay day.   Broughs Ltd, H.G. Ellis c1948 (2)

Payments for leading workmen's fire coal – Workmen residing in the village six pence a fortnight, all other workmen resident within 3 miles of a depot nine pence per fortnight.
                    Kibblesworth Lodge Agreement, 17th April 1923 (10)

Hugh Rowell at the Winding Engine of the Robert Pit.

Very few houses had a clock, so the time of day was signalled by the pit buzzer operated by the winding engineman. He sounded it at the start and finish of every shift and for bait times for the men who worked on the surface. The sound the wives dreaded was the three blasts sounded at 8.30pm which announced that the pit would not be working the next day.
     Bewicke Main, Harold Goodley
     1975 Ned Cowen's introduction
                    (1)

Started to sink the new pit Kibblesworth May 9th 1935 and finished sinking October 2nd 1935. The new pit is to be called Glamis. New pit holed into old pit November 24th 1936.
                    Urwin Notebook (1)

On Sunday the 4th September 1938 Kibblesworth Colliery Pit Head Baths will be open from 2pm to 5 pm for workmen and friends wishing to inspect the Baths.

After the first day go to work in your clean clothes, take them off in the clean locker room and hang them in your locker. Take your towel, soap and soap tray and go to your pit clothes locker. Put on your pit clothes there and leave your towel, soap and soap tray in your locker ready for your return from the pit.   Baths Opening Brochure 1938 (1)

The nationalisation ceremony at Kibblesworth Colliery occurred on Sunday when the Kibblesworth Silver Prize Band under Mr George Rodham led the parade round the village to the Glamis pit where the unveiling of a plaque and the hoisting of the National Coal Board flag by Mr Joseph Pratt a retired miner and one of the oldest residents in the village took place. The procession then visited the Robert Pit where the ceremony was repeated.

Gateshead Times, 10th January 1947 (3)

Hugh Wood and Co. Ltd or Huwoods made mining machinery and these photographs taken in May 1954 at Kibblesworth Colliery shows the PVC experimental conveyor belt on a GB40.

Mr Bainbridge (Manager at Kibblesworth Colliery) complained to the belt supervisor about the out bye belts and instructed they must have every joint changed and all bad belt removed as soon as possible. For forty eight hours this lad (I forget his name) never went home just stayed and carried on with the belt men each shift just changing the joints and belts as he had been directed.

The Life and Times of John Hutton Carr 1926-2009, 2010

John Hutton Carr was at Kibblesworth Colliery from 1968 to 1970.

This memento of a miner's friendship and relationship with his pit pony belonged to Joe Moore of West Pelton who died this year (2012). The pit pony replaced women and children in the coal mines. Since mine shafts were small and had low ceilings, it made sense to put small ponies into the mines. At the height of Pit Pony usage in 1913, there were seventy thousand working in the mines.

Clive was a pit pony in the Hutton Shaft Stables of the Robert Pit. In 1970-72 there were ten ponies on each shift 6.20-1.20pm, 1.20-8.25pm and sometimes up to three on 10.30-5.30am.

CLIVE
PUTTING PONY
KIBBLESWORTH COLLIERY
FEBRUARY 1974

At a special meeting on Tuesday the pit's union representatives agreed with NCB officials that the pit should close on October 4th. The 622 man pit has virtually run out of coal after 100 years of digging it. Whilst some of the older men will be redundant it is intended that alternative employment will be offered at other collieries in the area. Redundancy will be confined to men over 55. In an earlier reorganisation at the colliery this year about 100 men were transferred to neighbouring collieries.

Gateshead Post, 18th July 1974 (3)

The heart of a village stopped beating yesterday. For Kibblesworth Colliery, it was the end of the road and for the people whose homes stand in the shadow of the pit it marked the end of a 100 year association with the coal industry. Northern Echo, 5th October 1974 (1)

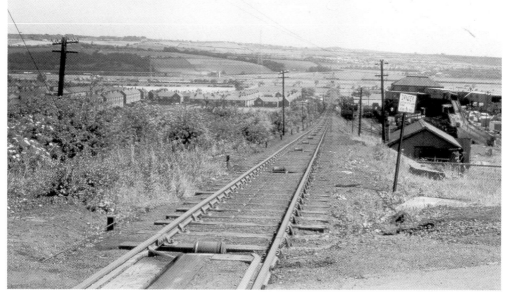

The Kibblesworth Colliery railway was opened officially on 30th May 1842 being an extension of the Springwell Railway. The original owners were Messrs J. Southern and Partners, but in 1852 the colliery was sold to Messrs John Bowes and Partners and the railway became part of the Pontop and Jarrow Railway which came into existence at the same time.
North East Industrial Archaeology Society Bulletin, 14th August 1971 (10)

The coal is conveyed to the depots and staithes by a system of main rope haulage, self acting inclines and locomotive haulage. The incline is 2,300 yards in length with an average gradient of 1 in 33 down which full trucks are lowered in sets of six by electrically driven rope haulage of 350 HP controlled by a dynamic braking system.

National Coal Board Report on Kibblesworth Colliery, No Date (1)

Only seven inclines remained in North East England at the beginning of 1974 and the closure of those on the Bowes Railway would leave only two. The final day Friday 4th October 1974 dawned wet windy and cold. The last coal left Kibblesworth at 9.30 am and the rest of the day was spent clearing out all of the wagons firstly from Kibblesworth and then from the inclines.

The Bowes Railway, Colin E. Mountford 1976

Part of the historic Bowes Railway line is to be preserved by Tyne Wear County Council. Council members many of who were shocked to hear that the National Coal Board intended to sell the train and lines for scrap metal, agreed to intervene. "It should be preserved," said Councillor Dan Marshall, "it is unique."

Gateshead Post, 17th October 1974 (3)

Chapter Four
The Chapels

The foundation stone for the Wesleyan Methodist Chapel was laid on Tuesday afternoon by Mr Ald Brown of Claremont House, Gateshead.

The bottle to be deposited was then exhibited and its contents read by the Rev. J. Dawson. The Rev. R. Haworth presented Mr Ald Brown with the silver trowel and the foundation stone was laid amidst much applause.

Chester-le-Street Times, 12th October 1867 (3)

Moved by Joseph Cook and seconded by Thomas Porter that we build a new Chapel. The new chapel to be built on the new ground and the old chapel to stand at present for the Sunday School and the cost of the new Chapel not to exceed £1200.

Wesleyan Trustees Minutes, 25th November 1910 (7)

The pitmen of Kibblesworth are turning their holiday (first ever national strike) *to good account. The men are clearing the ground that has been selected as the site of the New Wesleyan Chapel and are being assisted by many others representing various religious bodies. The use of the pit ponies has been granted free of charge and the work is proceeding quickly.*   **Illustrated Chronicle, 12th March 1912 (4)**

Mr L. Jobling of Birtley having obtained the contract for the New Church, operations have commenced this week. The hope of Kibblesworth Wesleyans will soon be realised. At the tea given last week by Mr J. Rowell and the concert which followed the sum of £9 was raised.   **Chester-le-Street Chronicle, 13th December 1912 (2)**

A report was given by the Secretary as to the Brick Money and it was decided that James Young, Roger Thew, Thomas Porter and Joseph Rowell gather the Brick Money in by July 12th. The Chapel Opening being the 13th July.

Wesleyan Trustees Minutes 28th May 1913 (7)

The new Wesleyan Church was opened on Saturday afternoon. The building which is of brick with stone facings is capable of seating about 350 persons and cost £1318, £900 of which has already been secured. The opening ceremony was performed by Mr G.A. Strong manager of Kibblesworth Colliery.

Chester-le-Street Chronicle, 18th July 1913 (2)

A most impressive memorial service was held on Sunday in the Wesleyan Chapel in memory of the men who fell in the Great War. Kibblesworth Temperance Band was in attendance parading the village and played a selection of  *sacred marches. Following the band was a good attendance of ex-service men showing deep respect to their comrades who had fallen. The roll call was then read each man's name being mentioned together with the cause of death. The total number who made the supreme sacrifice from the village was eleven.*

Chester-le-Street Chronicle, 19th November 1920 (2)

Kibblesworth Wesleyan Sunday School Football team for 1926-7 includes Back Row: Ben Ward, Harold Porter, Arthur Bell, Harry Reed, Jack Cook, Bill Gowland. Second Row: Tom Porter, Matt Riddle, ? Black, Hughie Fraser, Seymour Porter, Joe Cook, Joe Stott. Front Row: Harry Emmerson, Sid Porter, Jack Summerfield, Harry Richardson.

Resolved that we let the football club have the use of the vestry to hold a meeting on Tuesday night January 31st 9-10pm on the understanding that there will be no bad language used and no smoking allowed.

Wesleyan Trustees Minutes, 30th January 1911 (7)

The first wedding ceremony to be solemnised in the village took place on Saturday and to commemorate the occasion Mr T. Porter the oldest Trustee presented a combined Bible and hymnal to the bridegroom, Mr William Emmerson who married Miss Ada Maddison.
                    Chester-le-Street Chronicle, 11th June 1937 (3)

After Methodist Union in 1932 this became known as the North Methodist Church with the Primitive Church becoming the South Methodist Church.

Lance and Jim Madden of Gardiner Square in their cubs' uniforms taken on 13th February 1934. The group met at the North Methodist Church with Frank Madden as cub master. Jim was a senior sixer as can be seen from his arm bands. Both later were to become Scouts.

In Chester-le-Street, Stanley, South Moor, Craghead, the Peltons, Kibblesworth, Sacriston in every place where there are Boy Scouts in this district there will be left from house to house envelopes in which it is hoped to gather in much copper, more silver and many notes which will be sent to "The Chief" as we Scouts call him so that the Peace Ship he launched will be funded. The ship is manned by the boys of England. You will help won't you. Chester-le-Street Chronicle, 10th June 1938 (3)

45

Frank Madden was appointed the Scoutmaster of 1st Kibblesworth Group Registration number 15754 in the Chester-le-Street and District Local Association in August 1935 by a warrant signed by Chief Scout Baden Powell at Imperial Headquarters, London. The photograph was taken outside 34 Gardiner Square. The high coal ducketts, midden hatches and the tall wireless pole at number 35 are clearly visible. The bicycle came from the Co-op and cost three pound nineteen shillings and sixpence.

The interesting ceremony of laying the foundation stone of a new Primitive Methodist Chapel about to be erected at Kibblesworth was gracefully performed by Miss E.A. Spark of Darlington. They have

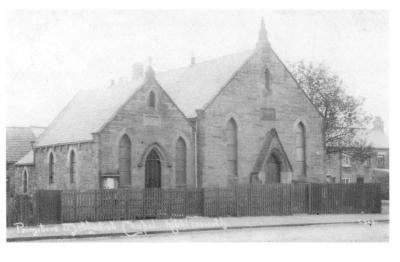

outgrown the old schoolroom in which they hitherto worshipped. The style employed in the new building is medieval Gothic and being situated on a high part of the village will prove quite a feature in the district. It is estimated that the cost will be about £300 of which £100 has been subscribed. **Northern Daily Chronicle, 12th August 1869 (4)**

Kibblesworth Colliery has often been visited with seasons of grace and the unstinted labour of the society has been rewarded.

Northern Primitive Methodism, W.M. Patterson 1909 (1)

The Primitive Methodist Sunday School Anniversary services have been held on the last two Sundays. The choir and children provided their usual programmes under the leadership of Mr J. Riddle the organist being Miss Boucher.

Chester-le-Street Chronicle, 17th July 1914 (2)

Kibblesworth Primitive Methodist Sunday School Anniversary will be held on Sunday 28th April 1918 conducted by Mr A.S.S. Ellis of Gosforth, morning at 10.45, afternoon at 2.00 and evening at 5.30. Collections will be taken at each service. Also on Sunday 5th May 1918 conducted by Mr John Shield of Gateshead. Scholars will recite and sing special music assisted by the choir.

Anniversary Leaflet 1918 (1)

Sunday School Anniversary at Kibblesworth South Church in the 1950s. Children include Joan Robson, Ann Pringle, Robert Wakefield, Bobby Robson, Penelope Coates, Joyce Rodden, Julia Reed and Linda Wilkinson. Joan Robson was later Head Teacher at Kingsmeadow Comprehensive School.

Everybody got new clothes for the Anniversary. Even when times were difficult, and work was short at the Colliery, still somehow or another all the boys and girls were spruced up and smart for the occasion. Ready to turn out for the parade through the village with the mobile organ to sing to every street some of the happy hymns they had all been rehearsing for weeks past.

Doon the Waggon-Way, James W. Madden 1989

A priests' paradise is tucked away in a derelict village church. There's wall to wall dog collar shirts, vestments, altar wine, chalices, candles and nativity figures. Hayes and Finch moved in to the Old Primitive Methodist Chapel in the late 1960s.

Evening Chronicle, 5th December 1979 (1)

Hayes and Finch was better known as "The Candle Factory". They closed in 2000.

The Chapel buildings are being converted into four one bed-roomed flats by Dr Ajit Jaiswal. He is keen to preserve the original standards of the chapel which dates back to 1869 changing little on the outside while adopting the inside to present use.

The Journal, 22nd February 2003 (1)

The North Church Sunday School Robin Hood production c1946
includes: Mr and Mrs Porter, Nancy Watson, Harold Porter, Roland
Rowell, Sheila Harker, Harry Emmerson, Anne Talbot, Ella Russell,
Joyce Porter, Elsie Emmerson, Alan Cook, Arnold Watson, Maurice
Bell, E. Brown, June Emmerson, Jean Porter, Ann Rowell, Linda
Eltringham, Elspeth Brown, Margaret Rowell, Margaret Gray, Pat
McConnell, Elizabeth Iveson, ? McGuigan, Audrey McConnell, Margaret
Curry, Jim Young, ??, Pauline Kay, Joan Peel, Mavis Peel, Glynnis Bell,
Kathleen Boggan, Thelma Brown, ??, Keith Emmerson.

*Mr and Mrs Syd Porter were the driving force (back row extreme left),
with the whole Sunday School as performers plus a few thespian adults
from the congregation, notably Harry Emmerson, the elderly blonde
fourth from the right, back row, and Roland Rowell, bowler hat, back
row, who regularly did a double comic act that usually brought the
house down (the old Church Hall).*   Arnold Watson, 2012

The Sunday School
Panto Aladdin and
his Magic Lamp,
1950 includes
Pauline Kay, Jackie
Peel, Kathleen
Boggan, Glynnis
Bell, M. Rowell,
Linda Eltringham.

1956 pantomine.

The pantomime Sleeping Beauty produced by Mr and Mrs S. Porter was given on Saturday in the schoolroom. Principal parts were played by Jean Rowell, Kathleen Boggan, Joyce Porter, Mary Wakefield, Willie Smith, Pat McConnell, Roland Rowell, Willie Farrer, Muriel Smith, Syd Rowell, J. Nairns, Malcolm Boggan, Margaret Boggan and Joan Wright. The junior members were dancers, soldiers and fairies. The pantomime was repeated on New Year's Day.

Durham Chronicle, 4th January 1957 (9)

North Methodists Messrs Rowell and Farrer, Mrs Cook and Dodds conducted the Bible classes on Tuesday. Preacher on Sunday was Mr H.G. Smith of Eighton Banks.

South Methodist Speaker at the Senior Christian Endeavour on Monday was Miss Reed of Gateshead. Duets were sung by W. Wilkinson and E. McMillan, leader was Miss Coates and reader Joyce Reed.

Durham Chronicle, 9th November 1956 (9)

The two societies joined in 1964.

Proposed by Mr J. Stott and seconded by Mr Roland Rowell that our new society shall be formed from the commencement of the April plan.

Leaders Meeting, 11th December 1963 (7)

On Saturday (7th December) in the presence of a large crowd of friends Mr and Mrs Lishman (Low Fell) performed the opening ceremony of Kibblesworth Methodist New Hall. Mrs Lishman turned the key and opened the door. Sunday School scholars Julia Reed and Trevor McMillan presented

Mr and Mrs Lishman with a bouquet and book token on behalf of the members. The Rev. G. Kemp thanked all who had helped towards "this great day." Durham Chronicle, 13th December 1968 (9)

In 2012 the Methodist Hall has been sold to Northern Print Solutions who have turned the building into a printing works employing a number of people from the village.

This Boys Brigade photograph includes: Ted Robinson, David Robson, Marc Kelly, Liam Gardner, Bob Bell, Paul Atkinson, Christopher Atkinson, Colin Clark, Les ??, Second Row: Douglas Hunter, Brian Kendal, Shaun Farrell, Brian Dawson, Ian Brewis, David Glister. Front Row: Glyn Hughes, John Noble, Mark Levington, ??, ??, Lee Bailey.

A sponsored Christmas word-search by twenty members of the 3rd Gateshead Boys Brigade raised £90 for the Leprosy mission. The Kibblesworth based brigade members had to find the links which a list of words had with Christmas and they were sponsored for the number of connections that they deduced correctly.

Gateshead Post, 16th February 1984 (1)

Chapter Five
The Schools

The quotes in this chapter are from Kibblesworth School log books (5)

Kibblesworth Colliery School was built by John Bowes and Partners to accommodate 193 children. The School log book commences on 10th May 1875 written by the first Head Master T. A. Craman.

The School was officially opened on 21st June 1875 by the Rev. Robert William Snape M.A. (Cantab.), Vicar of St Andrew's Lamesley. Messrs Mitcheson and Ironsides also present. Rev. Snape gave a short address to the children after which they were dismissed for a day's holiday. 25th June 1875

Attendance has fallen this week many infants being absent – this may be attributed in a great measure to the severity of the weather which has been extremely cold and damp. I gave a lesson on "Ants" to Second Class on Friday. Rev. Snape called.

18th February 1876

Thomas Arthur Craman resigned in June 1876. He later became the Head Master at Chester Moor Colliery School, south of Chester-le-Street, until his retirement in 1906.

The second Head Master was William Crosthwaite who commenced his duties in July 1876.

The attendance this week has fallen principally through an explosion at the Colliery. The Colliery is expected to be in working order next week and the following boys who work at it are attending School pro tem – John McLarnon, Andrew Martin, William Emmerson, James Kaye, Joseph Slavin, John Rowell and William Robson.

1st December 1876

This photograph was taken 5th March 1890 and shows Mr Crosthwaite (aged 27 from the 1881 census living at the School House, Kibblesworth) and either Miss Curry or Miss Alexander.

Some of the children are out this week gathering potatoes for neighbouring farmers: each farmer received a note of warning from the attendance officer. 1st November 1889

Many children are still absent gathering potatoes. 8th November 1889

Joseph Corker became Head Master in 1890. He is on the right of this photograph with Miss Margaret Armstrong Middleton on the left. The photograph was taken 22nd October 1897. Margaret had been a scholar at the school and then aged

13 years became a monitor in 1896. She later became a pupil teacher and was to remain at the school until 1921. Her brother William Fenwick Middleton was killed in 1916 and his name is on the War Memorial in the old school grounds.

Mary McMillan's attendance certificate – never absent and never late during the eight years ended 31st March 1918.

Joseph Corker retired in 1922.

During his 32 years connection at Kibblesworth School Mr Corker has never been absent. The Kibblesworth School has won the County Attendance Shield three times and under Mr Corker's leadership has proved one of the best attended school in the County of Durham. He has been a churchwarden of the Lamesley Parish Church for over eleven years and was a member of the choir for almost 30 years. On the eve of his retirement the scholars presented Mr Corker with a beautiful gold pendent, also a silver mounted umbrella.

Chester-le-Street Chronicle, 16th June 1922 (2)

Mr Stephenson and the winning School cricket team in 1938 in front of the Pavilion in the Welfare Park. Back Row: Gordon Hunter, Len Buckingham, George Taylor, Robert Drummond, Dennis Batey, Steve Ward. Front Row: Eddie Boggan, Stephen Winship, Jim Russell, Ken Potter and Kenneth Alderson.

Mr W. Stephenson, an assistant schoolmaster at Crook Council School has been appointed headmaster of Kibblesworth Council School. Trained at Armstrong College and has been at Crook since 1909. He lives a full and active life. He is a Wesleyan local preacher, until this season Secretary to Crook and District Schools Football League and Treasurer of the Crook Aged Miners Cup Competition.

Newcastle Weekly Chronicle, 16th September 1922 (4)

Taken in about 1925 this includes: Back Row: George? Kearney, George Watson, Jim Pratt, Dave Chambers, George Larch, Stan Reed, George Armstrong, Dave Boggan, George Symes. Fourth Row: Connie Farrer, Mr Jack Dobson class teacher, Lily Robinson, Ella Farrer, Connie Gowland, Barbara Clark, Mary? Potter, Rhoda Purvis, Winnie Potts, Barbara? Heslop, Annie Harrison, ? Goldsborough, Maggie Forster, Lydia Smith, Barbara Calvert. Third Row: Mollie Smith, Mary McNeal, Dora Potts, Alice Potts, Alice Richardson, Mary Lorraine, Betty Riddle, Ethel Porter, Agnes McConnell. Second Row: Jim Griffiths, Billy Lowery, Frank Madden, Norman Richings, Tom Rutherford, Tom Haughan, Jim Blades, Joe Tierney, Roy Tindall. Front Row: Ernest Young, Harry Woodhouse, George Winship, Joe Watson, Joe McMillan, Tom Morton.

Roy Dixon was appointed to the school in July 1948. This photograph was taken on the first of many school trips Roy went on over the years. Mr Stephenson is at the front with Roy far left.

Three teachers accompanied 59 scholars on an educational trip to the North East Coast today (9th July 1948), 30 children from classes 1 and 2 visited the Festival (of Britain) Ship Campania this morning. Mr Dixon and Mr Foster accompanied group, (7th June 1951). Mr Dixon took a party of children on the river trip down the Tyne (6th July 1976), J1 to Whitley Bay Mr Dixon and Mr McMillan (15th) J2 to Scarborough Mr Dixon and Mrs Gregory (16th) Mr McMillan and Mr Dixon took 20 children to Gateshead Stadium to see Great Britain v USSR Athletics match – Sebastian Coe running in the 800 metres (17th) All July 1981.

Mr Norman Seth became the fourth Head Master in December 1949. The staff photograph: Standing: Norman Seth, Hilda M. Aitchison (1947-54), Roy Dixon; Sitting: Elizabeth Proudlock, Miss I. Stokoe (1949-54). Miss Proudlock taught at the school from 1927 till she retired in 1963. Her speciality was Nature Study and she walked daily from Ravensworth Hill Head Farm Sunniside often arriving at school with examples picked from the hedgerows.

The study of Nature has been purposefully followed in the well cultivated school garden and in the immediate countryside. The children's notebooks testify in a striking manner to the success of this excellent training in first hand observation. School Report 9th and 10th September 1935

This series of photographs was taken in late 1953 or early 1954.

Back Row:
Colin
Shepherd,
Albert
Fenwick, ??,
Onsby
Taylor,
William
Ross, George
Logan,
William
Copeland,
Leslie Reay.
Third Row:
Winifred
Bradford,
Ann

Wilkinson, Christine Stewart, ??, Kenneth Eltringham, Peter McGuigan, Alfred Marr, Stuart Irwin, Joan Heatley. Second Row: Rita Howarth, Mary Lloyd, Linda Woodhouse, Muriel Watson, Frances Kennedy, Sylvia Blenkinsop, Eileen Bell, Jennifer Balmer, Linda Teasdale, Mavis Dunn. Front Row: Carol Wilkinson, Susan Woolmer, Dorothy Askew, Audrey Potts, Mary Temple.

Back Row: John Gardner, Denis Jackson, Allan Wilson, ??, ??, Alan Brown, Kenneth Moses, Ralph Wallis, ? Shand, Harold Murphy. Middle Row: Carolyn Shevels, Kathleen Atchison, Edmund Snowball, David Pine, Brian Harper, Alan Linton, Alan Stephenson, John Rutter, Ronald Irwin, Ann Southerland. Front Row: Pauline Thompson, ?? Bradford, Edwina Mason, Margaret Race, Linda Kennedy, Elsie Davies, Heallen Race, Nancy Bailey, Patricia Simpson, Jacqueline Richardson.

57

Back Row: George Potts, Ian McMillan, ??, Neville Hooper, Raymond Thompson, Alan Dodds, David Rutherford, Stephen Dewson, Edward Palmer, ??, Joseph Wright, David Murray, Malcolm Boggan. Third Row: Patricia Woolmer, Rodney Shevels. Second Row: ??, Kathleen Ekin, Bernard Moody, Terry Hughes, Peter Hillary, William Wakefield, Joseph Dodds. Front Row: Edna Bradford, Gwen Gowham, Freda Sewell, Christine Hesse, Brenda Rainbow, Sheila Snowball, Maureen Holyoake, Kathleen Makepeace, Margaret Iveson, Joyce Marr, Noreen Robson, ??, Gwynneth Pine.

Back Row; ??, David Hillary, Joseph Winnard, William Maughan, Ronald/Robert Irwin, ??, Laurence Gardiner, Thomas Wilkinson, Brian Bradley. Middle Row, Elizabeth Potts, Valerie Wilkinson, Ian Holyoake, Gerald Scott, ??, Michael Watson, Richard Watson, Sidney Blenkinsop, Joyce Wilkinson, Norma Larch. Front Row; Isabel Peel, Pauline Thompson, Jean Oliver, Susan McMillan, Vera Emmerson, Margaret Bradford, Jean Scott, June Reay, Shirley Palmer, Margaret Copeland, Joyce Richardson.

Back Row: Mr Seth, Geoffrey Scott, Thomas McConnell, Billy Wakefield, Leslie Bailey, John Thompson, Richard Rodden, Allan Brown, Dennis Lowe, Mr Dixon. Middle Row: ??, Anne Copeland, Margaret Dawson, John Nicholson, Frederick Bains, Roy Walker, Robert Reay, Terry Cuthbertson, Pauline Langdon, Doreen Irwin. Front Row: Margaret Oliver, Alma Fraser, Joyce McGuigan, Norma Whitfield, Dorothy Bradford, Patricia Pearson, Patricia Sewell, ?? Dawson, Florence Wiggins, Sheila Watson, Freda Davies.

Mr Seth had many health problems and he died in July 1957. Mr Samuel (known as Peter) Robinson had been a teacher at Kibblesworth School on at least two separate occasions and was appointed Head Master in January 1958.

The Head Master has had many years of experience of teaching in a variety of Educational establishments; he brings to his work a keen interest and an efficient administrative ability.
                    School Report, December 1958

The new council housing estate meant an expansion of school numbers. Six families with school age children moved into Moormill – Winnard, Watson, Murphy, Peel, Atchison and Dixon children were entered into the School Register

on the 8th January 1953 and that was just the start!. In April 1953 the total number of children was 124, by January 1954 the total was 179. On the 10th December 1956 new "prefab" classrooms were added in the schoolyard.

This morning Mrs Lowery reported to me that the Youth Club which met in the New Building last night were responsible for a broken panel of asbestos in the cloakroom wall. I reported this to Mr Brown and to District Office. Mr Dennison (District Office) stated that Youth work was regarded as being part of Education in the County and that the School building would have to be let to the Youth Club until such time as the young people had a place of their own.   7th and 20th March 1958

School Party includes – Back Row: Alan Wilson, Linda Kennedy. Front Row: Patricia Simpson, Kathleen Atchison, Edwina Mason, Elsie Davies, Helen Smith, Kenneth Eltringham.

December 14th Infants party. Parties in the Church hall – December 15th J1 and J2, December 16th J3 and J4. December 19th Carol Service in Methodist Church, the church minister Rev. H.R. Stafford took part. Following the service parents were invited to school to see the children's work.   December 1966

Dale Douglas and Tony McCartney photographed in the schoolyard in the 1960s. The badges include three Tudor Crisps (Tudor Crisps were a North East creation which had been launched and produced in Sunderland in 1947); Vimto drink, Mobil Oil and a Robertson golliwog badge.

Members of the Divisional Executive visited the school this evening (6.40pm) Head Teacher and caretaker both present. Purpose of visit was to inspect the building with a view to its possible replacement with a new school.   3rd July 1963

1972 Netball team. Back Row: Mrs Gregory, Iris Mitchell, Pamela Eltringham, Jean Poyzer, Mr McMillan. Front Row: Carol Simm, Janie Yates, Karen Lee, Sharon Dryden and Hazel Miller.

In September 1965 Emmerson McMillan became the seventh Head Master. Born in the village Emmerson attended the school as a pupil until he moved to Chester-le-Street Intermediate School at Bullion Lane. He transferred later to the Grammar School. Following teacher training at Leeds and National Service Emmerson started teaching at Springwell Junior School.

A most successful sports day was held with a good attendance of parents. The events were extremely well organised by the staff and at the conclusion the trophy was presented to the winning house  *by County Councillor R.W. Brown the chairman of the school managers who had donated the trophy to the school.* 12th July 1966

At the annual sports day County Councillor R. Brown presented the cup to William Winnard and Susan Hewitson captains of Armstrong House who had scored 143 points, Second Grainger House, Third Stephenson House, Fourth Collingwood House. Durham Chronicle, 11th June 1971 (3)

This photograph shows the site of the future new school.

Mr Dixon on course on Open Plan schools (7th September 1970), Mr Porter brought in plans of new school. (14th September 1970), Mr McMillan at County Hall re furniture for new school. (8th February 1972), Closing date for applications for Cook and Kitchen maid at new school (23rd June 1972), Managers meeting – interview applicants for new caretaker Mr E. Matthews appointed Mr S. Hornsby reserve (4th July 1972). Mr Matthews failed medical (September 1972).

Gary Arnold, Martin Fishwick, George Knox, Alan Dryden, Stephen Young, Stephen Saunders, Debra Wilkinson, Janet Wallace, Gillian Fishwick, Gillian Stacey, Janet Thurston, Diane Richardson, Lorraine Simpson, Gillian Scott, Avril Curry, Jacqueline Peel, Jean Turner, Thomas Winnard, Kevin Oliver, Trevor McMillan, Anthony Robinson, Stephen Fenwick, Jim Atkinson.

School Operetta Two Weeks to Californiay, Mime and School Choir – three nights at the Methodist Church Hall – Capacity audiences each night.   14th April 1970

1971 Paradise Island – Kenneth Bainbridge, Stephen Sanders, Stephen Simm, Jim Atkinson, Avril Curry, Lynn Griffiths, Janie Yates, Hazel Miller, Alan Dryden, Gillian Scott, Thomas Winnard, Trevor McMillan, Susan Hewitson, Alison Lowden, Melanie Wilkinson, Stephen Kendal, Alder Bradford, David Nichols, Kevin Oliver, Stephen Young, Martin Fishwick.

BBC Radio Durham visited school to record programme on the history of Kibblesworth.   5th July 1971

The school listened to a programme on Radio Durham which they had recorded before the summer holiday.   20th September 1971

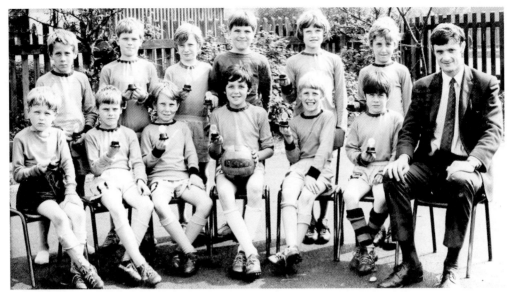

1969-70 Football Final Medals – Back Row: Stephen Young, Alan Dryden, Thomas Dodds, Trevor McMillan, Stephen Fenwick, Peter Summerfield. Front Row: Duncan McMillan, Ian Dryden, David Laverick, Anthony Robinson (Captain), Stephen Kendal, Ross Wilkinson, Mr Baker.

Autumn 1971 Infant 1 Teacher Mrs Ruddock (1956-62, 1965-81). Back Row: Robert Calder, Neil Pearson, Anthony Henderson, David McKenna. Middle Row: Amanda Dodds, Sue Corfield, Thomas O'Neil, John Prandoczky, Steven Watson, Geoffrey Douglas, Heather Mitchell, Julie Palmer. Front Row: Alison Wakefield, Robert Thompson, Brenda Harbottle, Carole Holyoake, Susan Kinghorn, Gillian Fenwick, Peter Young, Angela Fairlamb.

One more step along the world I go. (11)

Autumn 1971 Infant 2 Teacher Miss Medway (1971-73). Back Row: Colin Thurston, Roland Gallagher, Thomas Watson, John Fenwick, John Charlton, Anthony Wakefield, John Simm, Jeffrey Dennison, John Summerfield. Third Row: Deborah Palmer, Christine Knox, Gillian Dixon, Beverley Brownley, Allison Noble, Roslyn Morgan, Gail Brown, Victoria Emmins, Allison McMillan. Second Row: Rachel Gallagher, Elaine Bruce, Elaine Nicholls, Yvonne Elderbrant, Janet Atkinson, Marie Calder, Gail Lowden, Dawn Marshall, Helen Gale, Margaret Whitfield. Front Row; Thomas Fullard, Alan McAnaney, Thomas Laverty.

One more step along the world I go. (11)

Autumn 1971 Junior 1 Teacher Mrs Wilkinson. Back Row: William Bruce, Brian Dodds, Mark Brown, Paul Harbottle, Gordon Turnbull, James Marshall. Middle Row: Andrew Batten, David Hudspith, Graham Kendal, Robert Dixon, Anthony Whiteford, David Scott, Derek Hughes, Andrew Bruce, Malcolm Knox. Front Row: Brian Bruce, Karen Tindle, Michelle Thompson, Susan Bone, Joanne Healey, Dawn Wilkinson, Kathleen Whitfield, Susan Turner, Stephen Laverick.

From the old things to the new. (11)

Autumn 1971 Junior 2 Teacher Mr Dixon. Back Row: Alan Young, Paul Whittingham, Lawrence Fenwick, Michael Healey, Kevin Crossley, Stephan Prandoczky, William Evans, Robert Harrison.

Middle Row: Paul Bradley, David Stocks, Karen Knox, Deborah Simm, Janice Watson, Shirley Tasker, Stephen Bell, Kevin Summerfield. Front Row: Deborah Pearson, Dawn Lowden, Sonia Robinson, Denise Wakefield, Susan Wilkinson, Helen McMillan, Sheena Douglas, Lynn Bradford.

Keep me travelling along with you. (11)

Autumn 1971 Junior 3 Teacher Mrs Gregory. Back Row: Ross Wilkinson, Duncan McMillan, Alan Dodds, Kevin Bell, Ian Kennedy, Jeffrey Dodds. Middle Row: John Taylor, Anthony Nichols, Gary Liddle, Jeffrey Carthew, Michael Bradley, Ian Copeland, Ian Turnbull. Front Row: Edwina Miller, Jean Snowball, Rita Jobling, Sharon Dryden, Lynn Bridgett, Angela O'Neil, Kathryn Wilde, Janette Hewitson, Gillian Whitfield, Ann Laverick.

And it's from the old I travel to the new. Keep me travelling along with you. (11)

Autumn 1971 Junior 4 Teacher Mr Baker (1966-74). Back Row: Kevin Bruce, Alder Bradford, Michael Tindle, Thomas Dodds, Roland Dixon, Charles Graham, Kenneth Bainbridge, Murray Wakefield. Middle Row: David Nichols, Stephen Kendal, Kevin Simpson, Iris Mitchell, Jean Poyzer, Karen Henderson, Ian Young, Kevin Graham, Ian Dryden. Front Row: Gillian Summerfield, Hazel Miller, Beverley Janie Yates, Karen Laverty, Pamela Eltringham, Carol Simm, Melanie Wilkinson, Maria Evans, Jacqueline Dennison.

Round the corner of the world I turn. (11)

1971 Standing: Mr Baker, Tommy Dodds, Alder Bradford, Ian Dryden, David Nichols, Kevin Bell, Graham Kendal, Mr McMillan. Sitting: Ross Wilkinson, Ian Copeland, Ian Kennedy, Stephen Kendal, Michael Tindle, Duncan McMillan

League Cup Final –
Kibblesworth 2
St Cuthbert's Chester-le-Street 1. Ross Wilkinson and Stephen Kendal were presented with the trophy by Mr George Staines. 17th May 1971

In 2001 Tom Baker was awarded the M.B.E. for services to education in County Durham.

Back Row: Thomas Dodds (Katelo), Stephen Kendal (Officer), Ross Wilkinson (Tishtuk), Janie Yates (Astronaut). Front Row: Jean Poyzer (Nunuk), Hazel Miller (Ootek), Melanie Wilkinson (Atoka).

The Awkward Eskimo was performed at the Methodist Chapel Hall three nights with attendances of 146, 138 and 136.

15th, 16th, 17th March 1972

The £84,135 semi open plan new Durham County Council school at Kibblesworth replaces the original building built by the Bowes Company in 1875 and taken over by Durham County in 1905. The new school can accommodate 280 pupils aged between five and  *eleven. It has separate junior and infant departments divided by a multipurpose hall.*

*   Head Master Mr Emmerson McMillan, his staff of six full-time teachers and one part time teacher and 160 pupils moved in last November.*   Durham Chronicle, 11th May 1973 (3)

1973 – Joyce Scott, Nellie Larch, Emmerson McMillan, Nancy Boggon, Nancy Hall.

I am glad to be able to inform the Council that it is proposed to build a new school at Kibblesworth, where it is certainly very greatly needed. Dr Penfold Medical Officer of Health.

Chester-le-Street Chronicle, 18th September 1931 (2)

1973 – includes: Rachel Gallagher, Andrew Bruce, Jeff Dennison, Mrs Mitchell, Shirley Tasker, Paul Harbottle, Roland Gallagher.

Moved into new school. Wednesday 15th November 1972

The School was officially opened by Councillor Mr R.W. Brown. There were one hundred and three guests present. The Floral display was by Chester-le-Street Rural District Council. Mr Brown presented a bench seat to the school. 3rd May 1973

1973 – Deborah Simm, Ross Wilkinson, Mr Baker, Edwina Miller, Sharon Dryden, Kathryn Wilde, Jeff Dodds, Alan Dodds.

Because of the boundary changes the school is now transferred to the authority of Gateshead Metropolitan District Council.   29th March 1974

Pottery was a popular craft in the 1970s. The new school had a kiln and these items were typical of the work produced by children in the school.

Mr Hornsby, caretaker, discovered that the boiler house and the kiln room had been broken into. Minor damage had been done and a number of pieces of children's work had been taken. The Police were informed.   18th November 1974

The School Brass Band – Back Row: Graeme Brownley, Vincent Matthews, Paul Rowell. Front Row: Paul Hillary, Douglas Newton and Michael Wright.

The School held a Coffee Evening at which the children performed "Wizard of Oz", the Brass Band played and the children sang.

16th July 1979

Dawn Wilkinson, Debra Pearson, Karen Tindle, Pauline McCartney on left and Sonia Robinson, Beverley Brownley and Janet Atkinson on the right.

Mrs Gregory took a party of eight children to Barley Mow to give a demonstration of English Folk Dancing for a party of French Folk dancers.

15th July 1975

Silver Jubilee Celebrations many activities taking place in the school. The children had a sports day and also received crowns as a memento of the occasion.

June 5th-11th 1977

The Country Dancing Group. Back Row: Judith Bell, Julie Wright, Julie Palmer. Seated: Vivienne Stephenson, Carole Holyoake, Sandra Parmenter, Alison Hartshorn and Paula Baker.

English Dance Team and Choir at Birtley Carnival.   11th June 1977

The school went to the entrance of the M1 at Portobello to see Queen and Prince Philip passing.   15th July 1977

David Lister and Brian Kendal seen here with some of the many bottles found by the school at a local tip. (Photo courtesy of the Northern Echo)

The tip was first opened up by pupils during two digging sessions organised as part of their environmental studies. News that they had found a hundred and fifty bottles attracted older collectors and teenagers.
    Northern Echo, 13th March 1978 (1)

An exhibition was held in the School Hall in June 1978. Some of the School's collection of photographs can clearly be seen on these display boards. These photos have been used extensively in this book.

The exhibition was open for 3 days and there was an excellent turn out especially older ones very interested in old photographs. Photographers came from The Journal, Evening Chronicle and the Gateshead Post.
                                                                    June 1978

Emmerson McMillan getting the wet sponge from Paul Atkinson at the School Fair in the 1980s. Paul later moved to Birtley and in 1991 was killed in a friendly fire incident during the First Gulf War. Mr McMillan attended the funeral. Paul's name is commemorated locally at Kibblesworth, Birtley and Furrowfield School, Windy Nook and further afield in the Chapel Royal of St Peter ad Vincula at the Tower of London.

Infant 1 Class in 1983 with Mrs Betty Pearson (1981-87). Back Row: Anthony Wilkinson, Ian Cowey, Joanne Smith, Mark Gordon, Barry Gardner. Second Row: David Hall, Iain Palgrave, Jonathan Affleck, Ian Leather, Mark Baker, Mark Simpson, David Hartshorn, Sean Coffell. Front Row: Lynne Fenwick, Sonia Brotherston, Kay Bolton, Lisa Aynsley, Lucy Curry, Joanne Farrell, Emma McGurrell, Alona Newton.

More and more about the world I learn. (11)

Infant 2 Class 1983 with Mrs June James (1983-88). Back Row: John Noble, Lee Griffiths, Dawn Dacre, Glyn Hughes, Brian Kendal. Second Row: Brian Gardner, Darren McConnell, Lee Bailey, Allison Fenwick, Gillian Coulson, Christopher Copeland, Richard  Bennison, Mark Hetherington. Front Row: Alison Young, Nicola Wakefield, Judith Batey, Lesley Clarke, Brian Dawson, Shaun Farrell, Stewart Robson, Ian Brewis. In Front: Leo Fenwick.

All the new things that I see. (11)

Junior 1 class in 1983 were Roy Dixon's final class. He retired in July 1983 having taught at the school since 1948. Back Row: Zena Palgrave, Jayne Louise Stephenson, Sharon Whiteford, Jane Tinnion, Emma Simpson, Claire Fullard. Second Row: John Hall, Anthony Gardner, Alan Palmer, John Brownley, Christopher Atkinson, David Baker, Darren Marshall, Douglas Hunter. Front Row: Leigh Scott, Hayley Wood, Lesley Turner, Claire Devlin, Marie Atkinson.

You'll be looking at along with me. (11)

Junior 2 Class in 1983. The class teacher was Mrs Doreen Gregory (1960-84). Back Row: Ian Roberts, Colin Clark, Donna Elderbrant, Ian St Clair, John Copeland. Second Row: Alan Gardner, Shaun Turnbull, Jamie Davis, Russell Hughes, Michael Aynsley, John Wilkinson, Mark Hunter, Michael Bayne. Front Row: Nina Fairless, Claire Cameron, Lisa Copeland, Lisa Gardner, Jackie Wallace, Michelle Quinn, Kirsty Maguire, Michelle Coulson, Paula Coffell.

And it's from the old I travel to the new; Keep me travelling along with you. (11)

Junior 3 Class in 1983. The class teacher was Mrs Eileen Wilkinson (1971-90). Back Row: Paul Snowball, Edward Wood, Paul Atkinson, Beverley Gardner, Liam Gardner, Wayne Heslop, James Wood. Second Row; Kevin Eltringham, Scott Bradley, Marc Kelly, David Bayne, Craig Hartshorn, David Hunter. Front Row: Yvonne Allen, Melanie McGurrell, Marilyn Dennison, Lisa Whale, Joanne Parker, Pamela Robson, Dawn Matthews.

As I travel through the bad and good. (11)

The Stockwell Puppet Theatre visited the school but because of lack of facilities the church hall was used to which 174 children went. Afterwards Mr and Mrs Stockwell gave some good advice to members of the staff on puppetry. 24th April 1967

Alan and Brenda Stockwell and their puppet shows in the School Hall continued for nearly forty years. In 2000 Alan Stockwell was awarded an M.B.E. for services to education, a rare honour for a professional puppeteer.

Caretaker from 1972 Steve Hornsby retired in January 1990 and is seen here with Darren Eltringham and Stephen Crossley. Mrs Morrison then Mrs McAnaney worked as the caretaker's assistant. Betty Knox and Moyra Kendal were two long serving dinner nannies. Sid Parmenter took over as caretaker in 1990. He worked at the school until his retirement in 2004 when his place was taken by Andrew Batten a former pupil.

Infant 1 January 1990 teacher Mrs Dorothy Hall (1986-2005). Back Row: Richard Lowery, Richard Wilkinson, Nicholas Curry, Darren Eltringham, Anthony Young, Helen McCartney, Claire Anderson, Terri Hartshorn, Claire Thompson. Second Row: Cheryl Young, Gavin Brotherston, Andrew Forrest,  Stephen Crossley, Christopher Fuller, Michael Dunn, John Baker, Paul Clark. Front Row: Christopher Moysey, Ian Kennedy, Nicole Johnstone, Leanne Porter, Michaela Stanwix, Amanda Eltringham, Gavin Greenwell, Steven Lackenby, Andrea Hewitson.

Keep me travelling the way I should. (11)

January 1990 Infant 2 Teacher Mrs Christine Richardson (1984-96). Back Row: Christopher Lowery, Andrew Snowball, Kate Copeland, Louise Snowball, Emma Metcalfe, Michael Summerfield, Aimee Wilkinson, Emma Treeby. Second Row: Lucy Williamson, Kimberley Huddart, Natalie White, Mark Wallis, Rachel Stanwix, Nicola Anderson, David Robinson, Philip Hudson. Front Row: Stephen Forrest, James Batey, Cara Law, Donna Hudson, Rachel Copeland, Catherine Wilkinson, Julie Younger, Julie Lackenby.

Where I see no way to go. (11)

Junior 1 January 1990 Teacher Mrs Hilary Gibbin (1988-92). Back Row: Heather Dacre, Gemma Corbett, Daniel Wilkinson, Andrew Maguire, Helen Wilkinson, Scott Coulson, Amanda Dryden, Alison Shand. Second Row: Anthony Daly, Elizabeth Wilkinson, Stephen Hutchinson, Kenneth Stanwix, Natalie Hrisos, Andrew Hudson, Sean Porter,

Kerry Williamson. Front Row: Marie Smith, Tommy Affleck, Ross Cowey, Anthony Dixon, Barry Coffell, Graeme O'Boyle, Paul Charlton, Paul Fenwick. Dr Graeme O'Boyle is a scientist at Newcastle University researching the treatment of rheumatoid arthritis.

You'll be telling me the way, I know. (11)

Junior 2 January 1990 Teacher Mr Robert (Bob) W. Brown (1983-99). Back Row: Tracey McConnell, Christopher Wilkinson, Yannis Hrisos, Edward Moysey, Lindsey Roberts, Christopher Wade. Second Row: Bryan Dixon, Ian Fenwick, Kim Hewitson, Joanne Naylor, Ian Charlton, David Kennedy. Front Row: David Smith, Monique Hutchinson, Sonia Prandoczky, Ashley Brotherston, Natasha Johnstone, Joanne Coxon, Alistair Gowland, Craig Metcalfe.

And it's from the old I travel to the new: Keep me travelling along with you. (11)

Junior 3 January 1990 Teacher Mrs Edith Pullan (1990-94). Back Row: Mark Maguire, Joanne Robson, Tammy Smith, Rachael Weatherley, Christopher Roberts, Roger Wilkinson. Second Row: Christopher Thompson, Samantha Naylor, Luke Fairless, Layton Robinson, Craig Daly. Front Row: Claire  Coffell, Andrew Bennison, Angela Wakefield, Steven Brewis, Lesley Hunter, Neil O'Boyle.

Give me courage when the world is rough. (11)

Easter Bonnet parties were held for the two infant classes in the 1980s and 90s. Back row: Craig Treeby, Christopher McDonnell, Kevin Caiger, Michael Corbett, James Young, Paul Slee, Ian Wade. Front Row: Andrew Curry, Shaun Gallagher, Richard McQueen, Christopher Conway. The Juniors held decorated Easter egg competitions.

Back Row: Nicola Forrest, Sara Coxon, Jill Copeland, Kate Baker, Rachael Anderson. Front Row: Anne Marie Batey, Fay Brotherston. After a procession round the Junior classes there were games in the hall. The top class girls set out the tea in the Infant classrooms. At

the end of a happy afternoon the children paraded to the school gate in their hats.

The Gateshead Garden Festival took place in 1991. All schools in the Borough were encouraged to visit. Here Helen McCartney, Rachel Copeland and Ian Kennedy try their hand at tractor driving under the watchful eye of parent helper for the day John Curry. It was usually the mothers of Kibblesworth who came into school and helped out on a weekly basis and on trips. John Curry went to the Garden Festival and Edward Moysey came and helped Reception class children in the early days of BBC computers.

The all-conquering Badminton Team 1990-91. Standing: Mr McMillan, Luke Fairless, Tracy McConnell, Claire Kelly, Alistair Gowland, Mr Brown. Seated: Ian Fenwick, Angela Wakefield, Katie Dent, Steven Brewis

The school's badminton team left the opposition in the changing rooms. "They have won everything" said Mr McMillan, as he gave out medals by the handful.
Evening Chronicle,
July 1991 (1)

Robert W. Brown was appointed the eighth Head Teacher in 1993 following the death of Emmerson McMillan in December 1992.

The Gateshead Borough's Outdoor Centre at Dukeshouse Wood at Hexham was the highlight of the year for the older Junior school children.

Mr McMillan took 13 boys to Dukeshouse Wood Camp School for a week. During the visit they had outings to Lead Mines, Roman Wall, Hexham Orienteering and Warkworth Castle. 6th July 1979

Emma Morris, Claire Slee, Angelique Daniels, Samantha Caiger, Peter Matthews, Dionne Greenwell, Martin Fryer, Andrew Smith, Garry Kendal and Gemma Sebastinelli with the day old chicks at Hall Hill Farm, Satley in May 1995. Despite Kibblesworth being surrounded by countryside these visits brought the children into contact with many farm animals for the first time.

Judith Doran joined the staff as Deputy Head in September 1993. She became the ninth (and only female) Head Teacher in November 1996. The official opening of the Nursery Unit took place on 22nd June 2000. Pictured here are Judith Doran and

Councillor Mrs Minnie Robson, the chair of Governors who officially opened the Nursery.

2001 January Nursery Mrs Anne Hayes (1996-2001). Back Row: Georgia Matthews, Steven Little, Thomas Dixon, Keiran Brotherston, Daniel Spraggon. Second Row: Shannon Prandoczky, Teri Glasgow, Ashleigh Bruce, Lauren Watson, Jack Brunger, Nicole Quinn, Amy Appleby, Irish Greaves. Front Row: Jonathan Allman, Lucy Brown, Courtney O'Connor, Alex Wood, Charlotte Bushnell, Emily Ross, Sarah McCready.

Keep me loving though the world is tough. (11)

2001 January Reception Mrs Anne Hayes. Back Row: Gareth Brunton, Connor Tate, Megan Wood, Matthew Robinson, Sophie Carr. Front Row: Dominic Davis, Rhys Glasgow, Karl Knox, Samantha Major, Luke Coulson, Ryan Quinn.

Leap and sing in all I do. (11)

2001 January Year 1 and 2 Mrs Dorothy Hall. Back Row: Jordan Appleby, Amy McCready, Liam Watson, Shannon Wilson, Samantha Winnard, Joanne Simm, Amy Appleby, Lee Armstrong, Josh Hunter, Michael Leonard. Front Row: Paul Caiger, Jordan Keepin, Laura Brownley, Lauren Matthews, Bethany Pringle, Meg O'Neil, Natasha Bambro, Gareth Mitchinson.

Keep me travelling along with you. (11)

2001 January Year 3 and 4 Mr Stephen Fallon (1998-2003) and Mrs Carole Baker. Back Row: Lee Watson, Sophia Little, Dean Hughes, Laura Frank, Amanda Tunstall, Sarah Jane O'Neil, Kathryn Simm. Third Row: Jodie Pringle, Stephanie Kendal, Danielle Allman, Jordan

Gascoigne, Jordan Marshall, Christopher Mitchinson, Craig Urwin, Mark Gray. Second Row: Connor Wiseman, Connor Pearson, Andrew Dodd, Scott Major, Chelsea Appleby, Jessica Brunton, Rebecca Crossley. Front Row: Lee Gardner, Rachel Keepin, Michael Brownley, Daniel Harrison, Alan Dodds, Ben Hunter, Anthony Bruce.

And it's from the old I travel to the new: Keep me travelling along with you. (11)

2001 January Year 5 and 6 Mrs Jane Draper (1996-2002). Back Row: Melissa Gray, Samantha Parker, Ben Lumsden, Ethan Thompson, Daniel Smith, Kevin Dodds, Blu Greaves, David Dodds. Third Row: Kyra Marshall, Erin Gascoigne, Emma Morris, Paul Tunstall, Stuart Dobson, Paul Glister. Second Row: Alex Dunning, Hannah Johnsone, Toni Jade Taylor, Emma Southerland, Peter Matthews, Adam Young, Lee Wallace, Paul Hewitson, Mark Tracey, Dionne Greenwell, Sarah Winnard. Front Row: Jonathan Tindle, Lewis White, Dean Crossley, Paige Wilson, Claire Slee, Gemma McCready, Vicki Hudspith, Kenneth Johnsone, Craig Summerfield, Leanne Harrison. Absent Ashleigh Dodds and Steven Gardner.

You are older than the world can be; You are younger than the life in me. (11)

The Copeland family in Laburnum Crescent for many years provided the frog spawn for the Year 1/2 class in springtime. Sarah Jane O'Neil, Alan Dodds, Joseph Eltringham, Ben Lumsden, Charlotte Taylor, Michael Brownley, Leanne Harrison and Rachel Keepin are seen here when the class returned the froglets to the garden pond.

This salt dough Kibblesworth School boy was sold at the Friends of Kibblesworth Primary School Fair in the 1990s. It was made by one of the mothers Susan Hrisos. The Friends found all sorts of ways over the years of raising money to help with school trips and items required in the school not paid for by the Local Authority. Santa Claus was always at the Christmas Fair usually in the Hall recess and in later years the School had a real look alike Santa in Herbie Savory!

Henry the year 1/2 Hedgehog, hibernated in Autumn, woke up in Spring and ever so often went on walkabout in the North East. In 2002 he was found at the Angel of the North and in 2004 at Penshaw Monument. His sister Henrietta travelled the world with various children and adults. She went missing in Spain – so could be still trying to find her way back to Kibblesworth.

100% Attendance rosettes were introduced into the school in 1988. In 1994 Julie Younger followed in 2001 by Jemma McCready (far left) and in 2004 by Jodie Pringle (second left) were never absent during their time at the school. This photograph also shows Bethany Pringle and Dean Hughes who also received their 100% rosette and certificate in 2001.

Staff 2004-5. Joanne Beale, Fran Norie, Brendon Renwick, Jeanette Moysey, Middle Row: Andrew Batten, Sonia Brotherston, Carole Baker, Joan Cowburn, Jane Wright, Margaret Hunter, Moira Hogg. Front Row: Fiona Haddow, Rachel Brown, Year 3/4, Dorothy Hall, Year 1/2, Kevin Dodd, Head Teacher, Vicky Longhurst, Nursery and Reception, Craig Steele, Year 5/6.

Ever old and ever new; keep me travelling along with you.

And it's from the old I travel to the new: Keep me travelling along with you. (11)

Kevin Dodd became the tenth Head Teacher in September 2000. In June 2012 Kibblesworth became the first Primary Academy in Gateshead.

Chapter Six

The Community

*Everyone knows the best thing to come out of the mines is the
community.*   Durham Chronicle, 26th July 1974 (3)

Mr Parkin (*left*) and
an unknown man
beside the stone laid
by Mrs Ellen Pratt
(cost £5) in memory
of her husband John
Pratt.

*In glorious sunshine
and in the presence
of a large number of
spectators the
foundation stones of
a group of six Aged
Mine Workers'
Homes were laid last
Saturday afternoon.*

*Sir Alfred Palmer chairman of the directors of John Bowes and Partners
said he was glad that the cottages were to be built at Kibblesworth
because the men at Kibblesworth were amongst the finest in the country.*
                              Chester-le-Street Chronicle, 16th April 1926 (2)

*Only the cost of the material for three is being found by the Gateshead
district scheme organisers of the Durham Aged Mine Workers' Homes
Association, while the building of the whole six is being borne by the
colliery company Messrs John Bowes and Partners.*
                                            Unknown Newspaper, April 1926 (1)

There is no mention of an
official opening of the homes
as the 1926 strike started in
May and lasted to November.
The names of the first
occupants were added to
Chester-le-Street Rural
District Council's rate book
in January 1927:- William
Nutsford, George
Richardson, Henry Forster,
William Riddle, George
Rowland and George
Lowther.

During the 1926 strike the place was full of men and boys. Quoits were a great attraction. The men used to play on the spare ground beside the Post Office. They also dammed a stream where Gardiner Square is now and made an outside swimming pool. All through the summer the boys and men swam in that pool. Comic football matches were played to raise money for the strike fund.

Changing Kibblesworth,
Roy Dixon, Emmerson McMillan and Les Turnbull 1978 (1)

The soup kitchen was in the old hut and each morning hot cocoa was served. Several firms were very good in helping towards providing breakfast and dinner for the kids – mind just the children, nothing for the grown ups. The allotments beside the houses or scattered round the village on various patches of waste ground were a boon in those days.

Changing Kibblesworth,
Roy Dixon, Emmerson McMillan and Les Turnbull 1978 (1)

Both these groups are outside the Ex-Servicemen's Hut which was above the Aged Miners' Houses, with The Square behind them.

The Welfare Hall was officially opened by Mr A. Stott the managing director of Messrs John Bowes and Partners and Alderman J. Gilliland agent to the Durham Miners' Association. The building which cost about £3,500, is of  *imposing appearance and comprises games and reading rooms on the ground floor and reading and community rooms on the upper floor. Mr Stott and Alderman Gilliland each inseted a key at the same time and threw open the doors.*

Chester-le-Street Chronicle, 18th June 1937 (3)

The Kibblesworth Labour Party Women's section Christmas party includes: Mr Cuthbertson, Renee Abbot, Carol Rodham, Jenny Elcoat, Nancy Simpson, Lizzie Ward, Lizzie Taylor, Alan Brown, Rita Duffy, Irene Hudspith, Mary Brown, Minnie Robson, Frances Robinson, Elspeth Brown, Edie Cuthbertson, Dorothy Peel, Kathleen Atchison, Nancy Atchison, Theresa Beeby, Sylvia Blenkinsop, Michael Frith, Raymond Blenkinsop, Elizabeth Elliott, Kathryn Headley, Joan Robson, Dorothy Peel, Alma Smith and David, Bobby Robson, Freda Blenkinsop.

Kenneth Yeates was the village policeman in the 1950s. This pencil sketch shows also Barrack Terrace and the small bricks in the wall of the Old Hall. Other Police Constables included; R. Atkinson (959) 1948, H. Lancaster (808) 1949, B.P. Conlon (1033) 1949, Kenneth D. Yeates (967) 1954, D. Corfield (1962) 1969.

Kibblesworth's Luncheon Club celebrated its first anniversary in the Welfare Hall. To mark the occasion Mrs E. Curry the cook baked a first birthday cake and Mr Talbot had the honour of blowing the single candle out.　　　　　　　　　　Durham Chronicle, 15th October 1965

Kibblesworth Pit may have closed but it is business as usual at the Welfare Hall which is fully used by the local community. The levy payable to the management committee of the welfare scheme ceased in October and the dispersal of men from the area included the secretary and treasurer of the scheme. At present the hall is used by pensioners, local women's organisations, jazz bands and the library service.
　　　　　　　　　　Gateshead Post, 14th November 1974 (3)

By 1993 the Welfare Hall was in a dilapidated state and the site was sold for development. The children from the school were witnesses to the demolition.

　　Mr and Mrs John Soulsby incorporated the stones from the Welfare Hall doorway and the Foundation Stone into the garden wall of their house built on the site.

Kibblesworth Lodge banner showing Conishead Priory. The photograph was taken at the Welfare Hall left back: Joe Tunney, Bobby Frith, Tommy May, Will Forster, Joe Scratcher. On right back Jack Clough, Bob Beeby, Jack Winship, Jimmy Bryson, Matt Ward and Ralph Bell. In front: Billy Bowen, Will Young, (Pelton) Harry Patterson, Bob Cummins, (Treasurer), Charlie Pick, (Secretary) Joe Falloon, Jack Young, Ted Baker (ex-Bevin Boy), Harry Gibbons.

On Saturday the banner was carried round the village by Messrs J. Turnbull, M. Heslop, G. Hall, N. Robinson, R. Rowell, W. Watson, J. Loveday, J. Robinson and E. Baker. It was carried off the Race Course by T. May, J. Lowery, T. Marshall, C. Rippon, R. Hunter, J. Richardson, G. Black and W. Kane. Durham Chronicle, 21st July 1961 (9)

The Kibblesworth Band leading the way on Gala Day.

At the Borough Buildings Hartlepool on Saturday playing in the Fourth Championship Section they were placed second and qualify for the finals to be held at Belle Vue Manchester later in the year. This is a remarkable

performance in view of the fact that when the band was formed three years ago a large number of its members did not know a note of music. Gateshead Post, 14th March 1947 (3)

Billy Dawson and his father Bill are standing in front of the banner in the late 1960s.

Kibblesworth Lodge new banner was unfurled by Mrs Bessie Braddock M.P. for Liverpool West before a packed audience on Gala Eve. One side of the banner depicts a picture of the late Aneurin Bevan underlined with the words Unity is Strength and on the other side is a picture of Conishead Priory the Miners' Convalescent Home at Ulverston.

Durham Chronicle, 21st July 1961 (9)

The end of the road for Kibblesworth Miners' Lodge and their last appearance at the Gala. 1974. The photograph includes John Taylor holding his son John, Frankie Haydon and his wife, George and Rita Jobling, Arthur Jordan, Murray Wakefield, Pam Dawson, Steve Ward, Ted Baker, Rita Jobling, Ben Pick, Piper Richardson, George and Betty Storey, Bill Dawson, Brian Eltringham, Cyril Cook, Maurice Talbot, Jimmy Sampson, Maureen Jones, Jimmy Walker, David Wallace, Eunice Eltringham, Julie Rowell, Paul Rowell, Tom Dodds, Sonia Robinson, Erin Winnard, David Scott, Arthur Jordan, Lizzie Eltingham, Lawson Taylor and his wife, Michael McEnaney, Mrs Tasker, Nancy Watson, Freddie Potts.

Jimmy Walker (kneeling far right) was awarded the British Empire Medal in 1973. He had worked at the colliery from 1946 and had been Lodge Secretary since 1953.

An extensive recreation ground for the use of miners and their children provision of which has been made possible through the National Miners' Welfare Fund was opened at Kibblesworth on Saturday. The recreation ground has been placed in one of the most commanding positions of the picturesque mining village. A pavilion overlooks the terraced bowling greens and tennis courts while on either side of these are a football ground and a large amusement park for the children.

Chester-le-Street Chronicle,
5th April 1929 (2)

Lizzie Farrer, Betty McMillan and her nephew Emmerson at the Welfare Park in the 1930s.

Bowls – Includes Joe Urwin (centre), Ben Ward, Jack Cook and Mr Moses.

The annual supper and presentation of prizes in connection with the Kibblesworth Colliery Welfare Bowling Club took place in the North Methodist Schoolroom on Saturday night November 7th 1936 when a large number of members were present. Members of the Club had earned great praise through out the county. Messrs J. Hardman, J. Urwin and W. Alderson were presented with the cup and minatures of the Durham County Rink Competition.

Urwin Notebook (1)

Bowls: Norman Dobson (Grounds man), Tommy Wilkinson, Harry Porter, Vic Noble, Tommy Simpson, Bob Hedley, Joe Charters, Tommy Ferguson, Jim Talbot, Jim Fraser, Joe Hillary, Tommy Steele, Tom Gowland and Les Clark.

Kibblesworth Bowls Club have just completed a successful season in Section A of the NCB No. 6 Area Bowling League which they won quite convincingly. Durham Chronicle, 27th September 1957 (9)

Kibblesworth Welfare Cricket Club played in the North Durham Senior League.
Back Row: A.W. Graham, Treasurer, R. Armstrong, G. Armstrong, Alan Richardson, Jimmy Talbot, Arthur Bell, A. P. Benson, Harry Emmerson, Hon. Secretary.
Front Row: Mr J.F. Hunter, Vice

Chairman (Colliery Engineer), Lloyd Rodham, Tom Rowell, G. Watson, Jimmy Rodham, Jack Woodhouse, W. Henderson, Chairman.

The North Durham Senior League fixture between Kibblesworth and Pelton on the former club's ground which was abandoned on Monday was played on Tuesday night and resulted in an easy win for the home side. Pelton scored 131 for eight wickets batting only nine men. Kibblesworth knocked these off for the loss of five wickets. Rowell carrying his bat for 46 and Woodhouse 36.
Durham Chronicle, 5th August 1938 (9)

Cricketers include: Jimmy Fraser, Jim McMillan, Albert Rowell, Billy Brown, George Taylor, Willy Woodhouse, Jimmy Rodham and Harry Emmerson.

It called for a celebration dinner when Kibblesworth Colliery Welfare Cricket Club were presented with the No. 6 Area Trophy. Not since 1929 has the club won any honours. Dr J.C. Arthur and Dr Mrs K. Arthur made the presentation and each player received a replica and a new cap.
Durham Chronicle, 14th January 1955 (9)

This photograph was also taken at the celebration dinner and includes: Joan Hedley, Mrs Ekin, Mary Brown, Nellie McMillan, Ruth Morgan, Essie Brown, Carol Rodham, Daisy Johnson, Mrs Armstrong. Front: Mrs Hedley, Nancy Watson, Mrs Harry Emmerson, Mrs Bell, Mary Johnson, Esta Bell and

Lizzie Taylor. However, 1955 season was not as good for the cricket team.

Kibblesworth continued their sorry story when they were well and truly defeated by Eppleton in the Burn Cup by 67 runs. They gave a poor fielding display and even poorer batting. Kibblesworth tried to hit themselves out of trouble but catches were taken and at the end they were only 66 for seven.
Durham Chronicle, 9th July 1955 (9)

Back Row: Billy Tiplady, Maurice Bell, Raymond Briggs, Emmerson McMillan, Arthur Bell, George Smith, Stan Hedley. Front Row: Jack Smith, Albert Rowell, Willy Woodhouse, Jim McMillan.

Sacriston away to Kibblesworth Welfare team on Saturday in their North West Durham League fixture were just beaten by two wickets after an exciting struggle. At one stage they had victory within their grasp but a seventh wicket stand between W. Tiplady and E. McMillan saw both batsmen pass the 20 mark. Durham Chronicle, 25th May 1956 (9)

The 1950 gymkhana held in the Welfare Park with some of the Colliery buildings in the background. The lady riding the donkey is Lavinia Woodhouse.

Fourth annual pony gymkhana opened with a swing on Saturday when there were over 3,500 people in attendance in the brilliant sunshine which gave a feeling of festival. The entries included 264 ponies and 67 pit ponies. The farrier in attendance was Mr W. Thompson of Lamesley. Mr R.H. Harrison of Kibblesworth was secretary.

Durham Chronicle, 14th July 1950 (9)

Elspeth Brown – Miss Cadbury.

The first annual field day of Kibblesworth Colliery Miners' Welfare opened on Saturday with a fancy dress and comic dress parade headed by the Colliery Silver Prize Band. The parade consisted of eighty entrants attracted a large crowd of onlookers. Free teas were provided for 500 children and retired members and wives.

Durham Chronicle,
July 1952 (9)

This photograph shows prize winning budgerigars at Kibblesworth. The more popular past time was breeding and racing pigeons.

Over 150 guests were entertained to tea at the fourth annual function and pay out of Kibblesworth Homing Society. After a "grand spread" Mr Waller presented the prizes Mr J. Richardson carried off two cups, a salver and the bulk of the prize money. Mr Richardson is a stone man at Kibblesworth Colliery and devotes much of his leisure time to the training and care of his birds.

Durham Chronicle, 2nd November 1956 (9)

Darts:
Standing:
Norman May,
Dennis Batey,
Les Clark, Alfie
Dunn, John
Wakefield, Jack
Wakefield.
Seated: Stan
Ward and
Tommy May.

*Games
teams were
entertained at
Ferryhill Club
and were represented at darts by J. Wakefield, R. Robson, G. Peel, and J.
Bridgett, at dominoes by R. Smith, A. Kennedy, C. Burns and J. Tate, at
cribbage by A. Lloyd, S. Graham, E. Graham, G. Ward and at whist by
G. Hall, R. Temple, J. Duggan and J. Godbold.*

Durham Chronicle, 24th February 1961 (9)

The second birthday of the Labour Party Women's Section was held on
21st January 1955. Mrs J.A. Elcoat cut the cake. The photograph also
includes Mrs Huntley, Mary Brown, Bob Brown, Isa Young, Theresa
Beeby, Minnie Robson, Mrs R. Duffy, Mrs N. Atchison, Ted and Jenny
Baker, Katie Hedley, Essie Brown, Rene Abbott, Vera Makepeace, Lizzie
Ward, Babs Falloon, Lizzie Taylor, Freda Blenkinsop, Ned Cowen, I.
Hudspith, Mr Postle, Joe Makepeace, Mr Beeby.

Essie Brown, Alderman and local Durham County Councillor Ned Cowen and Rita Duffy with the new Kibblesworth Labour Women's Section George Tutill Ltd banner – bought in 1955 for forty eight pounds and five shillings.

Education Past and Present was the subject of Councillor G. Mathers talk to the Women's Section of the Kibblesworth Labour Party. Mrs A. Frith and Mrs Johnson were chosen to carry the banner on Gala Day.
Durham Chronicle, 18th May 1956 (9)

Fred Henderson is seen here with Brian Gardner, Jimmy McCartney, Kevin Lee, Pauline McCartney, Ann Percival, Denise Maguire, Linda Henderson, Karen Henderson, Keith Reed, Susan Abbott, Christine Abbott, Stephan Kendal, Christine Kendal, Karen McNeekin, Edna Archer, Rita Jobling and Jim Storey.

Kibblesworth Raven's Juvenile Jazz Band has been formed with over seventy members. The organising committee consists of Mr Henderson, Mr McGuire, Mr Hesse, Mrs McCartney and Mrs Brown. When asked about the band's hopes for the future Fred Henderson said: "We aim to win many cups and put the village of Kibblesworth on the map."
Durham Chronicle, 5th November 1965 (9)

Despite the bad weather which affected attendance the third carnival has been as successful as the previous two. The parade of ten visiting bands comprising 800 children was led by Kibblesworth Ravens through the streets of Kibblesworth to the Welfare Field.

Durham Chronicle, 6th September 1968 (9)

In the recent World Jazz Band Championships held in London Kibblesworth Ravens finished third overall in the world. There are 50 members of the Band. Gateshead Post, 7th September 1978 (1)

Taken outside the Welfare Hall at Kibblesworth the Ravens are wearing their tartan outfits.

Kibblesworth Ravens Jazz Band won the United Kingdom Championship at Great Yarmouth. The band scooped six trophies including drum major, mascot, bass drum, drum section bell lyre and best music. They were also best overall band. Gateshead Post, 13th November 1980 (1)

Lorraine Outterside said, "we got to travel all over the place. When we were at school we used to get mocked something rotten but the others didn't know what they were missing out on."
Gateshead Post, 17th December 1981 (1)

Kibblesworth Workmen's Club was officially opened January 14th 1956. Over the years the building has been extended and the steward's house built on the right.

At a presentation in the club last week Mr Syd Lavers chairman of the National Federation Breweries handed over the deeds to the secretary Mr J. Makepeace. Thirteen years ago six men: B. Brunskill, J. Peel, P. Atkinson, R. Hird, F. Tierney and J. Makepeace got together and decided to form a club.   Durham Chronicle, 8th March 1968 (9)

The Committee in 1956. Back Row: Gray King, Sam Urwin, Joe Walker, Jimmy Moses. Middle Row: Harry Rowntree, Jackie Redden, Mattie Dodds, John Willie Race. Front Row: Ronnie Hird, Bobby Beeby, Joe Makepeace, Tommy May.

Entertainment on Saturday was provided by the Four Rays and on Sunday by the Riversiders. On Thursday the club played host to the annual dinner for secretaries of the Gateshead and Felling District. Mr J. Makepeace was the host for Kibblesworth.   Durham Chronicle, 9th June 1962 (9)

As a young thinking club Kibblesworth created a bit of C.I.U. history when Rita Jobling became the first-ever woman doorkeeper around eight years ago (1980) and she is still welcoming members and visitors alike.
          Evening Chronicle, 14th November 1986 (1)

This photograph of the first outing of aged members of Kibblesworth
Workmen's Club to Seahouses in August 1957 includes: Cappy Watson,
Sam Foster, Charlie Pick, George Wilkinson, Robert Watson, Mr
Lumley, Jack Farrer, John Cross, Joe Moses, Ernie Elcoat, Jimmy
Cavender and Ernie Barnes.

*The Club's trip to South Shields was usually in the school holidays.
Thirteen double-decker buses would line up in front of the Club along
Rose Gardens. Each family was given a bus number. The children of
Club members were given pocket money to spend. The Club also held
Christmas parties.*   Pamela Mitchinson née Eltringham 2012

*The old people of Kibblesworth first felt Mrs Nora Gowland's presence in
1949 when she organised the first trip to Redcar and on that day the
lucky old people each received 26 shillings pocket money and a parcel of
sandwiches. The number travelling was about ninety.*
Durham Chronicle, 19th January 1961 (9)

Back Row: Connie Race, Katie Simpson. Middle Row: Mrs Gowland, Mrs Bailey, Mrs Gascoigne, Fred Potts, T. McNeil, H. Winship. Front Row: Lily Richardson, Dot Richardson, Mrs Griffiths (Policeman's wife), Hannah Shevels, Dorrie Potts, Mrs Lowther, Mrs Young, Mrs B. Pratt, Mrs Pratt.

Kibblesworth old people went to Redcar on their first free outing. Some of the committee members are behind some of the oldest – including Mrs H. Shields (77), Mrs F. Potts (80) Mrs C. Lowther (88), Mrs S. Young (88) Mrs B. Pratt (80) and behind were Mr F. Potts (82), Mr T. McNeil (80) and Mr H. Winship (83).   Northern Echo, 8th June 1949

Happy Senior Citizen trippers include: Mr Woodhouse, Lavinia Woodhouse, Nellie Armstrong, Jack Redden, Meg Eltringham, Jenny Elcoat, Frances Robinson, Lizzie Ward, Millie Winship, Katie Heatley, Meggie Baker, F. Linton, Mrs Crosson, Flo Young, S. Purvis, Mrs Race, Mrs Bryson, Mrs Brown, Mrs Rodham, Billy Lowery, Jack Summerfield, Katie Simpson, Jane Anne Farrer, and Mrs Grieves.

Terry and Tony Watson are well known throughout the village of Kibblesworth. Tony was a member of Gateshead Congress Harrier Club in his younger days. They have both been Lamesley Parish Councillors for over thirty years. For many years Terry was Chairman of Kibblesworth Workingmen's Club and was the National President of the C.I.U. until 2007.

Club members are organising a yard of ale contest and Easter Bonnet and fancy garter parades in four hours of fun and games to raise cash for a children's home in Wrekenton. Chairman Terry Watson said "the club adopted the home last year because a girl in the village works there in a voluntary capacity. Whatever funds we raise we give some of the money to them."

Gateshead Post, 31st March 1983 (3)

Mary McMillan, Gladys Palmer, Thelma McConnell, Jenny Dewson, Eva Forster, Josie Hall, Bella Boggan, Dot Richardson, Joan Shevels. In front Rachel Eltringham, Nellie Armstrong and Meg Eltringham at the celebrations following the Coronation in 1953 outside the large hut which was behind the Post Office. Most of these families lived in The Square.

Children at The Square's 1953 Coronation party included: Kathleen Atchison, Joan Heatley, Thomas McConnell, David Harper, Shirley Palmer, Carolyn Shevels and Jacqueline Richardson

School reopened this morning – Coronation souvenirs distributed then school dismissed for holiday.

Kibblesworth School Log Book, 1st June 1953 (5)

The Women's Institute 21st Party held in the Welfare Hall in May 1956 includes: Lavinia Woodhouse, Belle Stewart, Mary Wilson, Dot Richards, Nellie Armstrong, Esme Taylor, Mrs Spoors, Mary Fishwick, Ada Urwin, Dot Richardson, Rachel Eltringham, Hannah Emmerson, Harriet Taylor, Katie Hedley, Esther Laverick, Hilda Seedhouse, Mrs Peel, Meg Eltringham, Thelma McConnell, Mrs James, Mrs Hillary, Mrs Palmer, Mrs Grieves, Mrs McMillan, Olive Hedley, Mrs Russell, Dorothy Heslop, Mrs Brown, Mrs Barker Brown, Mrs Huntley, Meggie Alderson.

Nelly Armstrong, Meg Eltringham, Jane Ann Farrer, Milly Winship, Essie Brown and Lizzie Ward on a Women's Institute trip in the 1950s.

On Saturday members of Kibblesworth Women's Institute enjoyed their annual outing to Morecombe. At the meeting at the Welfare Hall the monthly competition was for the prettiest brooch and was won by Mrs Brown, Mrs Horne and Mrs Berry. The monthly prize was won by Mrs Urwin and Moody. Durham Chronicle, 15th June 1962 (9)

The Women's Institute's "Village Wedding" includes: Ethel Reed, Mrs Hedley, Mrs Farrer, Meg Eltringham, Nellie McMillan, Mrs Wilkinson, Mrs Marr, Betty McMillan, Mrs Russell, Irene Russell, Susy Warren, Vinnie McMillan, Nancy Boggon, Minnie Horn and Katie Hedley.

Fire gutted a wooden youth club at Kibblesworth yesterday. Damage was estimated at more than £1,000. The club building was built by members twelve years ago and plans were underway to extend the premises. "We are lucky the fire did not reach the new hut. When I got there the old hut was in ruins and it was very disheartening", said Thomas Bailey, assistant club leader. Northern Echo, 14th January 1970 (1)

Brenda Copeland, Maureen Murray, Frances Murray, Esme Whitfield, Mary Martin and Christine Ruddock – members of the Youth Club netball team.

Terry Watson, Albert Johnson, Tony Leahy, Tony Watson, Herbie Savory, with Suzy Russell environmental worker employed by Lamesley Parish Council. Ryan Quinn and Jordan Appleby are beneath the carving.

Kibblesworth Karvers was set up as part of Gateshead Council's Prime Time initiative which aims to encourage older people into the arts and has been running for over ten years. In a continuation of the Marking the Ways work they have been creating a number of stiles which distinguish the new footpath circuit to the north of the village. Kibblesworth Environment Centre opened in 2001. Staffed with its own community environmental worker the centre aims to work with local people to enjoy, sustain and improve the natural environment.

Marking the Ways in Gateshead Leaflet 2005 (1)

The Plough football team in the 1970s includes: Back Row: Keith Reed, Charles Copeland, David Nugent, Raymond Davison, James Shand, Anthony Robinson. Front Row: David Young, Jeff Kendal, John Ainsley, James McCartney, Alan Younger, Barry Robinson

The village of Kibblesworth took on a carnival air on Whit Monday when the members of the Plough Inn organised comic cricket match and fancy dress parade in aid of the old people's organisations. The match was opened by Tyne Tees Television announcer Michael Neville bowling to the Kibblesworth opener and with a ball not described in any book he got one of the home side lbw (leg before wicket).

Durham Chronicle, 15th June 1962 (9)

Emmerson McMillan, Chairman of Lamesley Parish Council with the newly erected pit wheel c1990. Lamesley Parish Council origins dates back to 1894. The pit wheel had been brought from Shildon Colliery and erected by the Parish Council.

Last week, children from Kibblesworth Primary School joined staff and contractors to give the wheel a coat of paint. Lamesley Parish Council has been working with housing company Frank Haslam Milan North-East and the Gateshead Housing Company to restore the monument. Heather Miller, from Frank Haslam Milan, said: "The wheel is symbolic to the village. By involving local schoolchildren, not only does it teach them the history of the village but they will also grow up to respect the area in which they live".
                                        Northern Echo, 12th July 2010 (1)

Lamesley Parish Council Gardening Awards in the 1990s includes: Back Row: Jack Patterson, Joe Elliott, Jimmy Atkinson, Ronnie Laverick, John Mastaglio, Mary Wilkinson, Sandra Snowball, Christine Hudson, Ian Wade (father). Second Row: Mrs Elliott, Dolly Patterson, Peggy Atkinson, Doris Laverick, Mrs Wood, Jarvis Coates. Front Row: Andrew and Philip Hudson, Ian Wade (son).

Chapter Seven
War Time

Kibblesworth Colliery's Roll of Honour from about 1917 lists one hundred and twenty nine men who are serving, missing or killed. In the 1990s Lamesley Parish Council refurbished the Roll and placed it in a new frame. The Primitive Methodist Sunday School Anniversary in 1918 included a hymn called The Roll Call (in memory of the Fallen Soldiers in the War) with these words:

There we'll meet the lads who left us,
At their King and Country's call,
They who fell in thick of battle,
Truly they were heroes all.

This Fancy Dress Parade took place during Wings for Victory week a national fund raising event held in the UK from 1st to 8th May 1943. Each county in Britain was set a target for the amount of money they should raise in order to contribute to the cost of an aircraft, which in turn would be named after the town or county which raised enough money. The parade includes: Emmerson McMillan, Minnie Brown, Nora Greaves, Doris Gowland, Margaret Talbot, Enid Emmerson, Winnie Coulson, Robert Thompson, Mary Lumley and Harry Brown.

Home Guard George Madden had served in the First World War in the 9th DLI and became a sergeant. He was posted missing in 1918 and was a Prisoner of War in East Prussia. Four of his sons served during World War Two.

After several Air Raid Drills it is found advisable to have only one playtime in the afternoon. Consequently in future the Infants will have playtime at the same time as the Seniors. Their timetables will be adjusted accordingly.
Kibblesworth School Log Book,
25th September 1939 (5)

The Air Raid Precaution (ARP) group taken at the Welfare Hall includes: Back Row: R. Hewitson, H. Watson, R.W. Brown, J. Gowland, Alan Linton, Joe Eltringham, J. Urwin, R. Armstrong, R. Harrison, Joe Russell, D. Urwin, O. Best. Front Row: W. Harker, J. Young, J. Richardson, Mrs Edna Gowland, Mrs Isa Young, Mrs Nin Nicholson, Mrs Ada Urwin, Mrs Linton, Mrs Reed, Bill Reed, Tom Crosson, J.W. Gowland.

Children present in the School shelters on account of an air raid alarm sounding just before morning assembly were marked as being present at school. Work was not begun till 10.15.
Kibblesworth School Log Book, 12th November 1941 (5)

Lancelot Gardiner Madden
Signalman Royal Navy
HMS Lapwing
20th March 1945

Joseph Wilkinson
Gunner Royal Artillery
Lapuan Malaysia
21st December 1944

The War Memorial built in the grounds of the old school, now The Millennium Centre, was dedicated on Saturday 13th August 2005.

The quiet village of Kibblesworth on the western slopes of the Team valley has a long tradition of community activities which were nurtured in former days by the sturdy mineworkers of the collieries and the strong fellowship of the two Methodist Chapels.

Dedication Booklet 2005

(1)

Valerie Kirkley, Joyce Scott, Kathleen Huntley, Alma Noble, and Dolly Patterson.

All who served their country in war time deserve the highest praise and those who died in the service of their country should have our everlasting gratitude. Dedication Booklet 2005 (1)

Back Row: Josh Hunter, Devon Proctor, Danielle Appleby, Aaron Proctor, Shannon Prandoczky, Mrs Dorothy Hall. Front: Dominic Davis, Amy Appleby, Sophie Taylor.

Where they played together as children they will now be honoured and remembered by future generations. Dedication Booklet 2005 (1)

Chapter Eight
The People

GEORGE RIDDLE, CASHIER.

Mr George Riddle the cashier of the Birtley Co-operative Society has now been appointed Secretary of the Carlisle Society. Born at Kibblesworth George Riddle went to work at the local pit but at the age of sixteen happened an accident which necessitated the amputation of his right foot.

Chester-le-Street Chronicle, 19th July 1912 (2)

George was elected to Co-operative Wholesale Society Board in 1923. He was President of the Newcastle Co-operative Congress in 1936. He was awarded the C.B.E. in 1937 and was knighted in 1942. Sir George Riddle died in 1944 aged 69 years.

Dennis Lowe at Chester-le-Street Grammar School in 1960.

Meet the man who is surely Gateshead's highest flying son – as well as the fastest flying. William Dennis Lowe a native of Kibblesworth is a member of the elite corps of Concorde pilots. His name will live forever in aviation annals for having piloted the first Concorde into New York on the 22nd November 1977.

Gateshead Post, 29th June 1978 (1)

But that was just the start. We know him today as Captain 'Jock' Lowe, the first man since Sir Sefton Brancker in 1929 to be President of the Royal Aeronautical Society and Master of the Guild of Air Pilots and Air Navigators, Concorde Chief Pilot and the world's longest-serving Concorde pilot, Director of Flight Operations for British Airways, lecturer, broadcaster and tireless cheerleader for aviation in all its forms.

General Aviation, October 2009 (1)

Four and a half years work by a Kibblesworth man has meant a new life for a swan. Mr Thomas Bryson-Smith, a retired Newcastle University instrument maker has spent his weekends giving the Bowes Museum silver swan a complete repair and overhaul so that the public will once more be able to see it in action. The main problem was that the swan's neck was broken and Mr Bryson-Smith has spent many hours dealing with the intricate workings of its mechanism. The neck has 300 moving parts. Durham Chronicle, 8th December 1972 (3)

In Changing Kibblesworth, Tom's mother Mrs Annie Bryson-Smith is named as the oldest resident in the village. Mrs Smith died October 1984 aged 102 years.

Kibblesworth Pearly – George Storey saw a photo of a Pearly King in London and thought why not a Geordie Pearly. Nearly a year later he had made his suit which has 6,025 pearly buttons on it, all by hand. He wears it to help to raise money for charity. Lamesley Chronicle 1975 (3)

117

Emmerson McMillan – a household name in Kibblesworth. As well as being head of Kibblesworth County School, he is also choirmaster (25 years) and assistant organist (30 years) at his local Methodist Church and is involved with well known choirs – Stanley Forum Men's Gospel Choir and Gateshead Festival Chorus. He teaches the guitar, recorder and clarinet and is proud of the success of his pupils at various music festivals.

Durham Chronicle,
30th February 1984 (3)

Mr and Mrs Fred Potts of 5 Short Row Kibblesworth who on Wednesday celebrated the 50th anniversary of their wedding at Lamesley Parish Church on November 2nd 1888 are to hold a family reunion on Sunday when their four sons, four daughters, twenty four grandchildren and twelve great-grandchildren will be present.

Chester-le-Street Chronicle, 4th November 1938 (3)

Mr and Mrs Frederick J. Potts of 5 Short Terrace celebrated their diamond wedding with their family and Mrs H. Foster a bridesmaid. Mr Potts had worked 52 years at Kibblesworth without losing any time.

Unknown newspaper, November 1948 (1)

Mrs Minnie Robson was awarded the M.B.E. in the Queen's Birthday Honours in 2004 for her services to the community of Kibblesworth, Tyne and Wear. Mayor of Gateshead in 1984, Borough Councillor for Kibblesworth, she was made an Alderman in 2003. Minnie received her M.B.E. from the Prince of Wales at Buckingham Palace. Granddaughter Karen Engle, great-granddaughter Joanna Engle and sister Elspeth Curry are pictured here with Minnie after the ceremony.

Joseph Falloon has been in the Union for twenty years and has acted as Pit Inspector and Average Taker. He has been Secretary of the T.U. Lodge at Kibblesworth Colliery for twelve months and is now its elected Chairman. He is a gardening enthusiast and Chairman of Kibblesworth Allotment Society.

Coal, November 1948 No 19
in a series of articles by
H.A. Freeth (1)

Joe Stott when asked the age of Kibblesworth Colliery scratched his head, and then told me that when dismantling an old pumping engine house some time ago he found a stone inscribed 1786.

Coal, October 1951
an article by Sid Chaplin (1)

Mr Stott aged 87 years had lived in the village all his life. He was engineer at the colliery and was connected with many organisations in the village including the Welfare Committee and Senior Citizens and was also president for a good many years of Birtley store. He was a lifelong member of the Methodist Church being a local preacher for 65 years.

Durham Chronicle,
1st December 1972 (3)

A member of one of the many families who moved to the new houses in the village in the 1950s local artist Laurence Gardner has produced a large variety of models including Cullercoats fishing women, Roman and Viking soldiers and miners.

At the official opening of the Millennium Centre, Princess Anne was handed a bronzed bust of a miner in a helmet sculptured by local artist Laurence Gardner – commemorating the area's mining past.

Evening Chronicle,
25th April 2002 (1)

Jim McMillan played for Crook Town Amateur Football Club from 1951 to 1967. He was a member of Crook's four post-war Football Association Amateur Cup winning teams, giving him the unique record of four winners' medals. There is even a McMillan Drive at Crook!

Born at Kibblesworth he went to the local school and moved at eleven to Chester-le-Street Grammar School where he played both football and cricket for the school. Jim is seen here with his England Amateur Football cap which he in got in the 1958-59 season.

Simon King (*left*), one of the Hairy Bikers, lived in Ashvale Avenue Kibblesworth as a baby. His father was one of the Club Committee members in 1956. His mother's great uncle Luke Potts' name was added to the village War Memorial in 2008. He is seen here with the other Hairy Biker, Dave Myers.

Hailing from the North-East, Simon King is a big, blond-bearded biker with an infectious laugh and bags of charm. This easy congeniality served him well for years in his work as a first assistant director and locations manager for film and television (including the Harry Potter series of films), but his passions lay elsewhere. A love of food was encouraged early by his family and particularly Si's father, who would bring back exotic ingredients from his voyages with the Royal Navy.

Northern Echo, 23rd March 2010 (1)

James Madden was born in Kibblesworth, lived at 34 Gardiner Square, attended the local school until he was fourteen and then left to work at Birtley. During the Second World War he joined the R.N.V.R. and became a Lieutenant. He was mentioned in dispatches. After demob Jim trained to be a teacher and taught at Heworth Secondary Modern School. With Gordon Hunter he was one of the prime movers in the effort to get Kibblesworth a War Memorial. He has organised the Remembrance Day services at Kibblesworth since the war memorial's dedication in 2005.

Professor Trevor McMillan BSc, PhD, Hon MRCP, Hon FRCR.
Trevor, the son of Emmerson and Margaret McMillan is the Pro-Vice-Chancellor for research at Lancaster University and Peel Professor of Cancer Biology.

It's easy to call him by his first name because he is nothing like the stereotyped academic egghead aloof, pedantic or impatient with ordinary intellect. A Geordie by birth he was brought up in a Durham mining village where his father was Head Master of the local school. He got his first degree at Lancaster, a first class honours in biological sciences.

The Guardian, 30th May 1997 (1)

Chapter Eight
Royal Visitors

On Wednesday the Duke and Duchess of York visited a number of collieries owned by Messrs John Bowes and Partners Ltd. They travelled via Birtley to Glamis Pit at Kibblesworth. This is the latest of the Bowes' mines and has been named after the Duchess of York's family.
Chester-le-Street Chronicle, 31st July 1936 (3)

The Duke and Duchess were received by Mr George A. Strong (Colliery Manager) and an unannounced function took place when the Duchess laid the foundation stone of the new Welfare Hall.
Chester-le-Street Chronicle, 31st July 1936 (3)

At the Glamis Pit Mr Strong conducted them to the Engine House where the engineer Mr E.H. Kirkup explained the winding gear to them. The Duchess, after a conversation with the Duke, asked if they might go down the mine and it was arranged for them to do so.
Chester-le-Steet Chronicle,
31st July 1936 (3)

White overalls and scarves were produced and the Duchess donned an overall and tied the scarf round her hair before the descent. The party submitted to the usual formality at the pithead of surrending matches and cigarettes before going down the shaft. Both the Duke and Duchess carried pit deputies' sticks. (Used for measuring coal seams.)
Chester-le-Street Chronicle,
31st July 1936 (3)

The Duke and Duchess descended 600 feet to the Busty Seam and then were conducted along the wagonway to the coal face where Bob Richardson and John Copeland two miners were working on an automatic coalcutter. The Duchess clambered over the coal to where the men were working and helped by one of the miners took a pick and hewed some coal. She carefully picked it up and placed it in her pocket for a souvenir. The Duke also hewed some coal.

Chester-le-Street Chronicle, 31st July 1936 (3)

The royal party visited a row of modern pit houses – Gardiner Square. After admiring a number of gardens in front of the houses they went on to the Welfare ground where the Duchess stopped for a while to peep at a sleeping baby the three months old son of Mrs Hilda Barnes.

Durham Chronicle,
31st July 1936 (9)

*At the miners'
bowling green the
Duke and Duchess
of York both
decided to try their
hand at the Game.
The Duke had
several shot under
the guidance of Mr
Joe Urwin but at
his last attempt
the bias took the
bowl right off its
course. "I'd sooner
have billiards"
said the Duke.
When the Duchess
was given a bowl by Mr John Cook she remarked that it was heavy but
she went on the green and sent it along towards the jack missing it by
only two inches.*   Urwin Notebook (1)

*It was then the turn of Kibblesworth schoolgirl Claire Kelly to present her
Majesty with a posy of roses, fuchsias and carnations Claire who was
wearing a dress made especially for the day. She had spent the week
practising how to curtsey in preparation for her royal task. "It's been so
cold standing around for so long but it was worth it," said Claire, "the
Queen said hello and asked me which school I was representing."*
Gateshead Post, 6th December 1990 (3)

The children from Kibblesworth School welcomed the Royal visitor in 2002.

Her Royal Highness the Princess Royal was originally due to open Kibblesworth Millennium Centre last October but her visit was cut short because of fog.

Evening Chronicle,
April 2002 (1)

The Millennium Commission awarded the village £499,000 in 1999 to convert the old school building dating from 1875 into an environmental and education centre for local people of all ages to use.

Gateshead News,
Summer 2002 (1)

Princess Anne speaking to members of the line dancing group outside the Millennium Centre.

Acknowledgements

To George Nairn who is so generous with his collection of postcards and photographs.

Carole and Paul Baker, Birtley Local History Society, John Hunter Carr, May Chapman, Enid Charters, Brenda Clark, Elspeth Curry, DAFT the Durham Amateur Football Trust and Sam Smith, Billy and Pam Dawson, Malcolm D'Northwood, John and Rosy Gall, Bob and Olive Harrison, Julian Harrop, Martin Hayes at West Sussex Local Studies Library, Fred and Mary Henderson, Doreen Jackson, James W. Madden, Jim and Anne McMillan, Trevor McMillan, Pamela Mitchinson, the Monday Coffee morning ladies, Colin Mountford, Jacqueline O'Boyle, Ted Robinson, Minnie Robson, Malcolm Smith, R.W. Standing, Alec Thompson, Steve and Nancy Ward, Arnold Watson, Harry Wynne and the North East Police Group.

The Chair and Governors of Kibblesworth Primary School now Kibblesworth Academy who allowed me to use the Kibblesworth Archive and School Log Books. (5) The Log Books are in Tyne Wear Archives 1875-1899, (E.KB1/2/1), 1899-1929 (E.KB 1/2/2), 1929-88 (E.KB 1/2/3).

The Kibblesworth Archive (1) – village and school photographs, collection of newspaper articles and cuttings plus any references in books and magazines to the village was begun by Roy Dixon, Emmerson McMillan and Les Turnbull for the book Changing Kibblesworth. It has been added to over the years and the files have been used as the primary sources for this book.

A Comparison of the Geographical Development of two mining settlements in County Durham, (Kibblesworth and Grange Villa) by Stephen Walker c1980. (6) In the Kibblesworth Archive.

Beamish Museum, Living Museum of the North, Photographic Archive, British Library Newspaper Reading Rooms, Colindale, Chester-le-Street Heritage Group Archive (2), Clayport Library, Durham (10), Durham County Record Office, Gateshead Local Studies Library (3) Newcastle Local Studies Library (4) Northern Echo – Chris Lloyd and Christine Watson.

Reproduced by permission of Tyne Wear Archives (7) Bewicke Main School Log Books 1900 E.KB2/2/1, 1931 E.KB/2/2; Kibblesworth Methodist Church Trustees Minutes C.KB2/1/1, Leaders Minutes C.KB3/2/1.

Reproduced by permission of Durham County Record Office (8) Chester-le-Street Licences PS/CS 42 (The Plough, Kibblesworth); an aerial view of Kibblesworth Village in 1947 (DCRO CC/X 172/7).

Reproduced by permission of the Advertiser series and Durham County Record Office (9).

D/WP2 Durham Chronicle 1904 (/49), 1906 (/51), 1936 (/75B), 1938 (/77), 1946 (/83), 1950 (/87), 1952 (/89), 1955 (/92), 1956 (/93), 1957 (/94), 1961 (/98), 1962 (/99), 1965 (/102), 1968 (/105).

One More Step by Sydney Carter – Reproduced by permission of Stainer & Bell Ltd, London, England www.stainer.co.uk (11).

Andrew Clark of Summerhill Books for all his help and support.